Thomas Applegate

**The Voice of Sacred Triples**

Thomas Applegate

**The Voice of Sacred Triples**

ISBN/EAN: 9783337145897

Printed in Europe, USA, Canada, Australia, Japan

Cover: Foto ©Lupo / pixelio.de

More available books at **www.hansebooks.com**

# THE VOICE

OF

# SACRED TRIPLES.

BY THE

REV. THOMAS APPLEGATE,

AUTHOR OF "SACRED GEOGRAPHY AND HISTORY," "FRUITS OF THE SPIRIT," ETC.

BOSTON:
PUBLISHED FOR THE AUTHOR BY
E. P. DUTTON AND COMPANY.
NEW YORK: HURD AND HOUGHTON.
1866.

RIVERSIDE, CAMBRIDGE:
STEREOTYPED AND PRINTED BY
H. O. HOUGHTON AND COMPANY.

# PREFACE.

THE triples of Holy Writ are associated with some of the most interesting features of the dispensations of God to man. Twelve comprehensive and important themes are discussed in the pages of this work. Each subject is distinct and independent of the rest, and designed to afford material for reflection " when sitting in the house, and when walking by the way." If the reader will take this volume with him in his sequestered walks, and make it the sharer of his temporary seclusion from the corroding anxieties of business, the triples which it aims to elucidate may serve to shed the perfume and lustre of the name of Jesus around his lone and pensive path, kindling his fervor, and disposing him to renewed devotion to his best Friend that "sticketh closer than a brother."

The Three Revelations of Christ embody appropriate thoughts for Advent and Christmas. The gaze of the Church has ever been fixed on the contemplation of Christ's coming — Christ come — Christ returning. Patriarchs and prophets caught far-off glimpses of Him on His earthward mission. Kings and priests reflected the kindling glories of the Sun of Righteousness, before He rose upon the world. They were His appointed forerunners, like clouds in the eastern sky, flushed by the breaking dawn.

The holy ministry points back to the Nativity as the central fact of the Bible, around which the history of the world has crystallized, and taken its shape; and it looks forward to that august era, when the Lord Jesus shall be "revealed from heaven," to judge the world in righteousness, and consummate the triumphs of His reign. The past, the present, and the future have an inseparable connection with Christ. Pluck His sacred name from the record, and the annals of our race are only a chaotic enigma, a maze without a clue. Preach Christ crucified, Christ risen, ascended, and glorified, and the mystery of the world's destiny becomes solvable; the ways of God are justified, and the actions of men have a light, and an aim, and an end that would otherwise be wanting.

The Three Temptations are drawn from the Gospel for the First Sunday in Lent; and though particularly applicable to that solemn season, will be found equally serviceable in confronting the enemy, on any occasion that he makes his attack.

The Marys at the Cross, and the Last Words of

Christ, belong to that class of subjects suitable for Good-Friday; but the holy lessons, which they inculcate, appeal to our hearts ever, with melting tenderness. The Three Ascensions, and the Three in One, will remind the reader of the goodly custom of the Church, in the celebration of Holy-Thursday and Trinity-Sunday. The field travelled over, in the range of these threefolds, is rich and suggestive. Important truths are latent in every theme; and the practical lessons are numerous and obvious. The writer regrets that he has brought so much feebleness and infirmity to the treatment of topics so interesting and instructive, and hopes that the Spirit of God will accept the effort, and give it usefulness in the Church, and the glory shall be to the Father, and to the Son, and to the Holy Ghost, three Persons in One God, world without end. Amen.

CORTLAND, N. Y., *September*, 1865.

# CONTENTS.

|  | PAGE |
|---|---|
| THE THREE REVELATIONS OF CHRIST | 1 |
| THE THREE SISTER GRACES | 29 |
| THE THREE JEWISH FESTIVALS | 50 |
| THE THREE SACRED MOUNTAINS | 70 |
| THE THREE LOVED ONES OF BETHANY | 105 |
| THE THREE CHOSEN DISCIPLES | 125 |
| THE THREE TEMPTATIONS | 145 |
| THE THREE MARYS AT THE CROSS | 162 |
| THE THREE DYING WORDS OF CHRIST | 179 |
| THE THREE ASCENSIONS | 200 |
| THE THREE MYSTERIOUS UNIONS | 216 |
| THE THREE IN ONE | 236 |

# THE VOICE OF SACRED TRIPLES.

### THE THREE REVELATIONS OF CHRIST.

"THE everlasting Son of the Father" made frequent visits to earth before He became incarnate. His delights were with the sons of men, to whom He vouchsafed His presence in angelic form as their counsellor and guide. When the venerable Abraham was at Mamre, sitting in the doorway of his Arab tent, enjoying the fresh breeze astir, he espied three men approaching him, two of whom were angels, and the third was the Son of God. The distinguished visitors partook of the patriarch's friendly cheer, gave renewed assurances of the birth of Isaac, and resumed their journey. St. Paul, commenting upon the incident, says: " Be not forgetful to entertain strangers: for some have thereby entertained angels unawares." The Angel of the Covenant conducted Abraham to an eminence that commanded an imposing view of Sodom and Gomorrah, and, pointing to those silent cities among the mountains, disclosed the startling intelligence that he was about to inflict on them a terrible destruction; because of the wickedness of the people. The patriarch interceded with impassioned earnestness for the guilty inhabitants, till he hoped he had won a reprieve. The illustrious speaker with whom he pleaded was Jesus Christ, who afterwards enunciated the solemn truth, "Before Abraham was, I am." "Your Father Abraham rejoiced to see my day: and he saw it, and was glad." "No man hath seen God at any time; the only-begotten Son, who is in the bosom of the Father, He hath declared Him."

There occurred another remarkable manifestation of deity one memorable night, in the history of Jacob. Between him and his brother Esau there existed a long standing grudge about the birthright; and tidings reached him that his offended brother was coming against him, on the morrow, with four hundred armed men. Dejected and anxious, the patriarch betook himself in the extremity to the God of Bethel, and felt in the ardor of his devotion a mysterious conflict, as if a person were wrestling with him, "twisting, thrusting, straining, and striving to hurl him to the ground." The assault came from no enemy. His opponent was the second person in the adorable Trinity. "And Jacob called the name of the place, Peniel, the face of God; for he said, I have seen God face to face, and my life is preserved." Thenceforth his name was no more called Jacob, but Israel: because as a prince he had power with God, and with man, and had prevailed.

The burning bush at Horeb was a singular phenomenon, outshining in brilliancy the blaze of noon. The fire occasioned no consumption of the leaves and branches, but reflected them with beautiful transparency. And when Moses turned aside to see this great sight, it became vocal with instruction. The Lord spoke to him, " out of the midst of the bush, and said, Draw not nigh hither: put off thy shoes from off thy feet; for the place whereon thou standest is holy ground. Moreover He said, I am the God of thy father, the God of Abraham, the God of Isaac, and the God of Jacob." But for the assurance of the voice which addressed him, the astonished Hebrew might have concluded that the supernatural exhibition was in some way connected with the revelation of an angel. Now, he was favored with indisputable testimony that it was Jehovah Jesus, the mysterious, incomprehensible One, who afterward conducted the exodus by a pillar of cloud by day and fire by night, supplied miraculously the migratory hosts with manna from the skies and water from the rock, and of whom it is recorded, " They did all eat the same spiritual meat; and did all drink the same spiritual drink : for they drank of that Rock that followed them : and that Rock was Christ."

To Moses Christ revealed Himself as a Prophet like unto him, that should rise in Judea; to Job, as the living Redeemer, who should stand in the latter day upon the earth; and to the patriarch Jacob, as the Shiloh, who should come in Judah's line. Balaam, in his blindness, had dim glimpses of the Messiah under the image of a star; and with the composure of one who reposed his confidence on God, uttered, as the Lord had taught him, the wondrous prophecy: "I shall see Him, but not now: I shall behold Him, but not nigh: there shall come a Star out of Jacob, and a Sceptre shall rise out of Israel." The sublime vision of Isaiah, exhibiting Jehovah as "high and lifted up, whose train filled the temple," was a manifestation of the glory of Christ. The Son of man, whom Nebuchadnezzar, king of Babylon, saw walking with the three Hebrew youths, in the midst of the burning fiery furnace, was the Son of man, who came to seek and to save them that were lost. The Ancient of days that appeared to Daniel, was the Infant of days, born in a stable at Bethlehem. We recognize, under every modification of development, the self-same Revealer of the Father, the self-same Head of the Church, the self-same Saviour of our race, who is Christ, the Lord.

The Augustan Age brought in the fulness of

time, when "God's blessed Son was manifested, that he might destroy the works of the devil." The event is referred to, in Holy Writ, as a mystery. "Great is the mystery of godliness: God manifest in the flesh." It is so regarded in our admirable Litany; "By the mystery of thy Holy Incarnation. By thy Holy Nativity and Circumcision." His assumption of our nature was an arrival from another sphere,— an incident in an existence that had no beginning. Christ could speak of a life that He had spent elsewhere. He could say, "I came out from God." "I came forth from the Father, and am come into the world." "I leave the world, and go to the Father." "His goings forth were of old, from everlasting." The children of faith must not pry into the hidden secret, but rejoice in the Advent, till the Lord shall lift the vail, and exhibit the inscrutable mystery as a subject of the clearest vision.

If it be asked, Why was so long a period allowed to elapse between the bestowment of the promise of the Messiah, and its actual fulfilment? it is sufficient to reply, The world was not fitted, by its population and general condition, to receive him earlier. Christ came thus late, that scoffers might find no excuse for their unbelief. There was as much propriety in the delay, as there is in not permitting a minor to come into the full possession of the property to which he is an heir. "The heir," says the Apostle, " differeth nothing from a servant, as long as he is a child, though he be lord of all; but is under tutors and governors until the time appointed of the father. Even so we, when we were children, were in bondage under the elements of the world: but when the fulness of time was come, God sent forth His Son, made of a woman, made under the law, to redeem them that were under the law, that we might receive the adoption of sons." "The fulness of time" was the best for introducing the Saviour and His Gospel. The minds of men were more at rest, and better prepared to detect Him, if He had been an impostor. The Jews were under the Roman yoke, and looked to the Messiah as their deliverer. He was a bright star in their horizon, and they were disposed to scrutinize

His claims with the nicest accuracy. The authorities of the Roman government were jealous of losing any portion of their influence, and were prepared to investigate His character with equal vigilance. The policy of both parties was to dispute everything they met with, and to admit nothing without proof. Christianity threw down the gauntlet, and challenged the closest research. The collisions that ensued served to rub the diadem into brightness, and to manifest to the world that Christ was certainly "He that should come, and that they need not look for another."

The aspect of human affairs had not looked so favorable for the Advent at any previous period. Men had been unwittingly preparing the way of the Lord, and making His paths straight. The nations of the earth, which, only a few centuries before, were in a state of internal antagonism, had become consolidated into one empire; and an appeal to Cæsar was deemed a sufficient protection in almost every capital and village of the habitable globe. The Romans had constructed Appian ways, and opened up arterial roads, thus forming paths for the Gospel to track its course over the known world. The Greek language, the noblest, and the grandest, began very much to dominate and prevail; and this constituted an appropriate vehicle, in which to embody and transmit the glad tidings of salvation, in the most expressive and permanent shape. Such were the happy results of the movements and changes of four thousand years, — the stirring of the waters, prior to the descent of the angel to impregnate them with the element of universal health. When the world was thus at peace, and the blessings of civilization were diffused, and the people were expecting a deliverer, and the nations were accessible to the feet of them that publish glad tidings, Christ came, — the Sun of Righteousness arose, — the Gospel of the Son of God was announced, — the national cistern became a world-wide fountain, and the Jerusalem lamp was superseded by the bright Sun in the sky, for the benefit of the race. The word of love and mercy went forth as the day breaks; and where it poured its meridian splendor, it eclipsed all light in its surpassing lustre. Its voice was more powerful than thunder; its echo softer than the summer breeze. It was whispered in the East, and rolled round to the West. It is repeated in the West, and rolls back to the East. It is gentle and fructifying as the spring shower; vivifying and enlightening as the sun; glorious and eternal as the heaven to which it leads.

The restrictive process, to which Deity had recourse, in selecting the nation of the Jews, the tribe of Judah, the family of David, and the Virgin Mary, to manifest the Godhead in human form, led him also to determine that the little town of Bethlehem should be the predestined and distinguished locality. "But thou, Bethlehem Ephratah, though thou be little among the thousands of Judah, yet out of thee shall He come forth unto me that is to be Ruler in Israel." The town of Bethlehem was indeed of little celebrity among the thousands of its neighbors, remarkable neither for elegance, nor commerce, nor the number of its inhabitants; but aggrandized by an event that will render it illustrious in the annals of eternity.

The residence of Joseph and Mary is the obscure village of Nazareth, in the province of Galilee. They are accustomed to repair to the synagogue to hear the Law and the Prophets, and sing the songs of Zion. And the soul of Mary, encouraged by the announcement of the angel, rises to heaven in the tuneful inspiration of her own splendid Magnificat, " My soul doth magnify the Lord, and my spirit hath rejoiced in God my Saviour. For He hath regarded the low estate of His handmaiden : for behold, from henceforth all generations shall call me blessed. For He that is mighty hath magnified me : and holy is His name."

To consummate the wondrous affair agreeably to ancient prediction, the Roman Emperor, as if moved by a special decree of Heaven, determines to take a census of all the people in his dominions, and requires them to appear for enrolment at the head-quarters of their respective families. The lineal descendants of David must present themselves in David's city. Joseph and Mary must undertake a journey to Bethlehem. They found the city much crowded, full of buzz and excitement. And as they could obtain no accommodation at a public inn, or in a private lodging, they were glad to avail themselves of the humble retirement of a stable. "And so it was, that while they were there, the days were accomplished that she should be delivered. And she brought forth her first-born son, and wrapped Him in swaddling-clothes, and laid Him in a manger."

> "Cold on His cradle the dew-drops are shining;
> Low lies His bed with the beasts of the stall;
> Angels adore Him in slumber reclining,
> Maker, and Monarch, and Saviour of all."

The starry night is lit up with unusual brilliancy. The air is filled with music from the skies. Angels sing in strains of inimitable sweetness, "Glory to God in the highest, and on earth peace, good will toward men." Sweeter and softer melody never fell on the ears of humanity.

Shepherds who were watching their flocks in the fields saw a radiance at midnight of more than earthly light, and heard the flutter of angels' wings. "And lo, the angel of the Lord came upon them, and the glory of the Lord shone round about them; and they were sore afraid. And the angel said unto them, Fear not: for behold, I bring you good tidings of great joy, which shall be to all people. For unto you is born this day, in the city of David, a Saviour, which is Christ the Lord." The shepherds were probably among the number of those who were looking for redemption in Jerusalem, silently musing at that moment when the kingdom of God should come, sighing, in the language of David, "O, that the salvation of God were come out of Zion." And "they said one to another, Let us now go even unto Bethlehem, and see this thing which is come to pass, which the Lord hath made known unto us." They told Joseph and Mary what it was that brought them, explained the angels' visit, caught a glimpse of the new-born king, and returned praising the Lord for the abundance of His mercy. Ever after, they would tread those fields as hallowed ground. If they slept, it would be in expectation of some fresh revelation, starting at imaginary sounds, fancying that an aërial orchestra was floating by.

The Saviour's birth was signalized by an unaccustomed orb, that gleamed in the pathway of the heavens. The Star of Bethlehem shone. Its brilliancy gave presage of a new and glorious dynasty. The wise men of Arabia and Chaldea were on the look-out for it. They had scanned with keenest search the radiant maze. They had made sure of every speck of light, though ever so small. And when the stranger star crossed their field of vision, and travelled westward toward Judea, they followed its guidance to Jerusalem, and inquired, "Where is He that is born King of the Jews? for we have seen His star in the east, and are come to worship Him." They evidently understood the connection between the sign and the circumstance, and were anxious to attest the birth of the illustrious personage, and do Him homage. The star that disappeared during their continuance in the Holy City, resumed its brightness when they left it, and, conducting the visitors to Bethlehem, drooped so low, as to single out the house where the young child was. The star pointed out the Star. The starry orb showed "the root and the offspring of David, the bright and the morning-star." The supernatural phenomenon died out above that humble dwelling as the Magi entered it; and they, opening "their treasures, presented the Holy Jesus with gifts; gold, frankincense, and myrrh." These were the richest offerings it was in their power to make. And these tangible and substantial proofs of their sincere devotion were not more the promptings of love, and joy, and grateful adoration, than the fulfilment of what David and the prophet Isaiah had before declared: "The kings of Tarshish and of the isles shall bring presents: the kings of Sheba and Seba shall offer gifts." "They shall bring gold and incense; and they shall show forth the praises of the Lord." "The Gentiles shall come to thy light, and kings to the brightness of thy rising."

But the precious things of earth belonged to Christ before the Magi presented them. "For all things were made by Him." He made the woman of whom He was born under the law. The star that shone over Bethlehem was an emanation of His own true light. The angels that announced His birth were His ministers to do His pleasure. The cattle that fed in the manger, where He was cradled, were His legitimate creatures; and the herbage, on which they subsisted, He caused to grow. "The gold and the silver are the Lord's, and the cattle upon a thousand hills." The clear cool waters that filled the sea of Tiberias were poured from His sacred hand; and the blasts that stirred them to their depths, and rolled the tumultuous billows to the shore, were hushed by His "Peace, be still." The foundations of Tabor and Olivet, and the mountains round about Jerusalem, were all laid by Him. And as He walked up and down the earth, He could recognize in its rocky ribs, and in all its adornments, the nice adjustments and familiar strokes of His own Almighty hand. The volcano's burst, the upheaving earthquake, the roar of ocean, the thunder-peal, and the howl of the tempest were the workings of His own energies, and He listened to them as the echoes of His own voice. The flowers that smiled in the opening spring He painted. The rainbow that decked His cloudy chariot He pencilled. The light that spread around Him was His mantle. The darkness that covered the landscape was His pavilion. What need of offerings to a being of such boundless affluence, whom our services can neither enrich, nor our wants impoverish? Does not the Lord require the heart? Will He not be better pleased with the warmth and fervor of our affections than with the sweat of our brow, the toil of our hands, the gold of our purse? The sophistry of this species of reasoning comes from an evil heart of unbelief, in departing from the living God. The grateful, joyful, loving soul asks, "What shall I render unto the Lord?" and forgets not gifts of gold, frankincense, and myrrh.

The several gradations of human condition were open to the Saviour's acceptance, and of these He chose the lowest. The varieties of earthly splendor were, in His estimation, only as so many degrees of littleness and insignificance. When He came down to earth, He came not to a throne, nor to ease and elegance, but to the cot of a poor carpenter. When He might have spoken to His Father, and commanded the attendance of legions of angels, He chose for his confidential associates twelve poor fishermen. When He hungered, instead of calling to His aid the stores of heaven, He partook with His disciples of their homely fare. "They gave Him a piece of broiled fish, and of a honey-comb." What an instance of the condescension of the Son of God! Only love, pure, perfect, disinterested, and eternal, could brook such a painful ordeal. If God so loved the world as to give His only-begotten Son, the Son so loved our race as to give us Himself. "This was compassion like a God." It comprised all gifts in one, and was so liberal as to preclude the possibility of its being ever said, that God could give us more. "Beloved, if God so loved us, we ought also to love one another." "God is love, and he that dwelleth in love dwelleth in God, and God in him."

The birth of Christ was the earnest of the world's redemption. It was virtually its accomplishment, revealing justice and mercy, and wisdom and power, in the sweetest form of manifestation. The highest angel never saw so much of God before. It is probable that up to this time the angels had only obscure intimations of the plan of redeeming love. The cherubim that bent over the ark seemed to denote, by their attitude of desire to look into these things, that God had not fully revealed to them His great purpose of mercy. St. Paul speaks of the manifold wisdom of God, now made known by the Church, unto the powers and principalities in heavenly places, as something to which the highest created intelligences were strangers, till they saw the Son of the Eternal stoop to clothe Himself with the habiliments of mortality. The amazing discovery was made the joyful occasion of gratulation and praise. If Christ had come to us differently, or suddenly and unexpectedly, we should have been slow to believe that His embassy was fraught with such kindly results. "But

God sent not His Son into the world to condemn the world, but that the world through Him might be saved." The Nativity is a theme of overflowing consolation and exquisite tenderness. It brings thoughts of a precious Saviour, and angels and men rejoice together in the glad history of His love. The doubts which some insinuate whether the twenty-fifth of December be really the day when Christ was born are of little moment. It is the day which Christians, from an early period, have chosen to observe as such, and it accomplishes every purpose which any other day could answer, in the celebration of the festival. It unites upon itself, through a long observance, the hearts of the faithful all over the world, and comes down to us with such pleasant memories, and blessed services, that it would be a shock to the sensibilities of Christendom not to follow this goodly custom of the Church, with the burst of grateful acknowledgment, "Thanks be unto God for His unspeakable gift."

The grandest revelation of Christ is destined to be realized in the splendors of the last day, when He shall come again in His glorious Majesty, to judge both the quick and dead. The unreserved disclosure, which He will then make, was explicitly taught, both by the Lord Himself, and His apostles. "The Son of Man shall come in His glory, and all His holy angels with Him; then shall He sit upon the throne of His glory; and before Him shall be gathered all nations." "Ye shall see the Son of Man coming in the clouds of heaven, with power and great glory." "Hereafter ye shall see the Son of Man sitting on the right hand of power, and coming in the clouds of heaven." The language employed in the Apostolic Epistles is equally emphatic, affirming the second advent to be preëminently a *revelation* of Jesus Christ. "Wherefore gird up the loins of your minds; and be sober and hope to the end, for the grace that shall be brought unto you at the revelation of Jesus Christ." "The Lord Jesus shall be revealed from heaven, with His mighty angels, in flaming fire, taking vengeance on them that know not God, and obey not the Gospel." "The Lord Himself shall descend from heaven with a shout, with the voice of the archangel, and with the trump of God." Passages of this complexion show the terrible contrast between the previous revelations of Christ and the one which will close up the series. *Then*, His glory was veiled, and the world knew Him not: *now*, He comes robed in the majesty of the Godhead, and the heavens and the earth flee before Him. *Then*, a tiny star guided to the spot where He lay: *now*, the sun, moon, and stars are merged in the intenser splendor of the glory that excelleth. *Then*, He was seen by only a few: *now*, "every eye shall see Him; and all kindreds of the earth shall wail because of Him." *Then*, He was revealed as the Son of Mary: *now*, He comes clothed with the all-sustaining power of Deity to judge the world in righteousness, and minister true judgment to the people. *Then*, He stood at Pilate's tribunal: *now*, Pilate must appear before the judgment-seat of Christ. *Then*, His voice was heard in the feebleness of infancy: *now*, it pierces the deepest charnels, causing all in their graves to hear the voice of the Son of God, and to come forth. Cemeteries of rock, and monuments of bronze, rend and explode, and pour forth their buried tenantry to meet the Lord. The sleeping dust in cathedral-tombs, and vaults of churches, and beneath the green turf, are simultaneously quickened and rise to give an account.

The scenery of the judgment is graphically painted by St. John, in the twentieth chapter of the Revelations. There is no human language half so magnificent. Oratory, rhetoric, poetry, and imagination are all beggared by its simple grandeur. "And I saw a great white throne, and Him that sat on it, from whose face the earth and the heavens fled away, and there was found no place for them. And I saw the dead, small and great, stand before God; and the books were opened; and another book was opened, which is the book of life, and the dead were judged out of those things that were written in the books, according to their works. And the sea gave up the dead which were in it; and death and hell delivered up the dead which were in them; and they were judged every man according to their works." Toward that huge assembly of immortal beings the most rigid justice characterizes every procedure, and not one solitary tongue dares to arraign the equity of the Lord.

The faithful in Christ Jesus anticipate the solemn transactions of that day as the only prospect worthy of their hope. The day of judgment is the day of their coronation, when they will receive their "perfect consummation and bliss, both in body and soul, in" Christ's "eternal and everlasting glory." They are described as looking for His advent, as the return of a conqueror, the coming of a friend, "looking for and hastening unto the coming of the day of God;" "Looking for the Saviour;" "Looking for that blessed hope, the glorious appearing of the great God, and our Saviour Jesus Christ." Whether He descend upon the lightning's wing, or, the eddying air, at mid-day, or at midnight, they know that when Christ, who is their life, shall appear, they also shall appear with Him in glory. "It doth not yet appear what we shall be; but we know that when He shall appear we shall be like Him: for we shall see Him as He is." Our frail bodies of dust, and death, shall be "changed, and made like unto His glorious body; according to the mighty working whereby He is able to subdue all things unto Himself."

> "Array'd in glorious grace,
> Shall these vile bodies shine,
> And every shape, and every face,
> Look heavenly and divine."

This comes of having our life hidden with Christ in God; our hearts linked to His by a living faith; our natures renewed by the Holy Ghost; our sins washed away in atoning blood; our souls robed with Christ's spotless righteousness, and Christ formed within us the hope of glory.

Look on the picture as sketched by the master's hand, and say which is the most pleasant and attractive, the dread approach of the grim king of terrors, or the glorious appearing of the Lord from heaven? The moment that the clouds shall waft Him from the throne, on which He now sits, within the range of the earth's attraction, the curse shall be extinguished, and death shall be swallowed up in victory. The dead of many thousand years, that fell asleep in Jesus, shall rise to greet Him. The saints, who are alive and remain, shall be caught up together with them in the clouds to meet the Lord in the air, and so shall they be ever with the Lord. "Then shall the righteous shine forth as the sun in the kingdom of their Father." The clouds of infirmities and reproaches, that now assail them, shall drop to the earth, as they ascend to the skies. And when the purity, and beauty, and blessedness on the right hand of Christ shall be seen in contrast with the dreadful array on the left, it shall be acknowledged that the salvation of the redeemed exceeds the most glowing descriptions that have been uttered concerning them. The splendor of that one scene will combine the consummation of all the plans of time, and the glories of eternity. This fabric of a globe, on which men have so fondly doted, shall be enveloped in one vast conflagration. All this wonderful exhibition of grandeur and minuteness, beauty and sublimity, adaptation and counteraction, shall be reduced to ashes. The brightest and noblest productions of man shall be consumed in the general fire. Trophies of victory, monuments of genius, cities and palaces, temples and statues, bridges and triumphal arches, shall melt like wax in the red flame. "The earth also, and the works that are therein shall be burnt up."

The promises of God shall receive their full and final accomplishment. Much as they may have been slighted, and called in question, and denied, that day will fix the seal upon them all. The Saviour's injured name shall be vindicated; His just rights asserted; the nations shall bow before Him; "His enemies shall lick the dust." "Wherefore, beloved, seeing that ye look for such things, what manner of persons ought ye to be in all holy conversation and godliness." "Be diligent that ye may be found of Him in peace, without spot and blameless." Trim the flickering lamp; nerve the trembling arm; lift the drooping head. Let your loins be girded, and your lights burning. "Be ye also ready, for in such an hour as ye think not, the Son of Man cometh." " Blessed is that servant, whom his Lord, when He cometh, shall find watching." Yet a little while, and He that will come, shall come, and will not tarry." Ponder much upon the scene. Meditate on the appearing of Jesus Christ.

> " The Lord shall come, the earth shall quake,
> The mountains to their centre shake,
> And, withering from the vault of night
> The stars shall pale their feebler light.
> Can this be He, who wont to stray
> A pilgrim on the world's highway,
> Oppress'd by power, and mock'd by pride,
> The Nazarine ! the Crucified ?
> While sinners in despair shall call,
> Rocks, hide us; mountains, on us fall;
> The saints ascending from the tomb,
> Shall joyful sing, The Lord is come."

## THE THREE SISTER GRACES.

THE three beautiful sisters, Faith, Hope, and Charity, have some features of resemblance in common. Faith has something of the expectation of Hope, and Hope something of the desire of love. Faith justifies the soul at the bar where the Law condemns. Hope lifts it above the dark and dismal shadow of mortality. And love animates it to run the heavenly race, till it shall win and wear the crown incorruptible. Like the colors of the rainbow, they maintain their distinctions, yet melt and soften into each other, by almost imperceptible degrees.

The beauty of this triplet has furnished the Arts with one of the most exquisite subjects for the exercise of human skill. Poets have sung the praises of Faith, Hope, and Charity; the painter has exhibited the Holy Three, in all the glowing colors of his pencil; the sculptor has carved them in the pure, and almost breathing forms of his marble; and the orator has made them the ornaments of a powerful and stirring eloquence. The excellences ascribed to them has called forth many kindly feelings, and kindled a taste for the sublime and beautiful.

The eldest sister of the group is *Faith*. She is superhuman. She comes down from above, and is the gift of God. She deals with the spiritual, and herself is spiritual. She has to do with the divine, and herself is divine. She believes God's word, trusts in His Son, and beholds the invisible. She leads us to Jesus, and by her gentle and persuasive influence disposes us to put our whole trust and confidence in His mercy, and receive from His fulness, and grace for grace. Her province is to discover to us the surpassing worth and preciousness of Christ; to enrich us with His unsearchable riches, and to make us one with Him, and He with us.

"Faith is the substance of things hoped for, and the evidence of things not seen." This is the definition given of it by St. Paul, in his

Epistle to the Hebrews. It receives and uses as substance whatever the Saviour, in the plenitude of His mercy, has promised to bestow. If we read, "I give unto my sheep eternal life, and they shall never perish, neither shall any one pluck them out of my hand;" "Ask and ye shall receive, seek and ye shall find, knock and it shall be opened;" these are promises which we enjoy as substance; and this substance becomes a reality, when that reality is wanted. Just as certainly as the promissory notes issued by a bank are equivalent to their value in cash, on account of the confidence which we repose in the directors, so faith in Christ, who is immutably faithful, is the substance of those ardent longings, which He has excited in our hearts, and the evidence of their realization, present and to come. The action of faith uniformly requires some promise as the basis of operation; otherwise, it would lose its character, and become daring presumption. When the Israelites were about to pass through the Red Sea, they were emboldened with the promise of God's protection to go forward fear lessly. To the Egyptians no such promise had been made; and therefore it was not faith, but presumption, on their part which led them to venture in pursuit, so reckless of the result. The faith, that leans upon an Almighty arm, finds a promise for every condition, a helper in every emergency, a soother for every sorrow. This is the intrinsic gold, that procures all blessings, and enriches with all good. Nor, is it simply one single act of the mind, but a series, a repetition of acts, forming the habit of believing, that constitutes faith. It is this that gives a distinctive character to the Christian, and makes him a believer. He lives, he walks by faith. "The life that he lives in the flesh is a life of faith on the Son of God, who loved him and gave Himself for him."

There is a divine unity in faith, which distance of time and differences of opinion, are powerless to affect. It continues essentially the same in every age of the Church, and all over the world. As the glorious sun, which now flings abroad his golden beams, is the same that shone on Eden's bowers; that veiled his face in sackcloth at the crucifixion of the Saviour, and that illumines all creation, so the faith that now pulsates in the breast of the lowliest believer, is the faith once delivered to the saints, and which inspired in the minds of our first parents a glorious hope, when God revealed to Adam the promise of Christ. It is denominated in Holy Scripture precious faith, — precious in its nature, precious in its object, and precious as the product of the Spirit. The trial of faith is more precious than gold that perisheth, though it be tried with fire, and will be found unto praise and honor and glory at the appearing of Jesus Christ. The sweet singer of Israel had tested its power to sustain the mind in the hour of the severest trial, when he said, "I had fainted unless I had believed to see the goodness of the Lord in the land of the living." The prophet Habakkuk could sing amid the wintry blasts of adversity, "Although the fig-tree shall not blossom, neither shall fruit be in the vines; the labor of the olives shall fail, and the fields shall yield no meat: the flock shall be cut off from the fold, and there shall be no herd in the stalls; yet will I rejoice in the Lord, I will joy in the God of my salvation." O wondrous faith that sees light in darkness, blessing in calamity, and discovers cause for triumph in the dreary and saddening scenes of our checkered pilgrimage. To her far-seeing eye the matchless, peerless One is all in all. She sees majesty in His meanness, dignity in His condescension, honor in His humiliation, and glory transcendent in His cross. She looks to Him as the wounded Israelites, in the wilderness, looked to the brazen serpent for healing and life. She looks upon Him as invested with surpassing loveliness, the object of supreme affection, deserving the warmest adoration that human hearts can offer. The look reflects back the radiance of His countenance, and transforms us into the same image from glory to glory, by the spirit of the Lord.

It would seem as if it were nearly impossible to award to so useful a grace too high a distinction. But Faith, divine as she is, affords no substitute for the Saviour. She is only a mean to an end, — the instrument of salvation to bring us to Christ, to be saved by His righteousness alone. The ship riding in the roads heaves not her anchor to fetch the little boat from the shore, but throwing out a line, bids the frail vessel grasp it, and draw itself to the ship. The Lord Jesus, who is in heaven, says, "Him that cometh unto Me I will in no wise cast out:" and inviting us to lay hold of that promise, assures us that we shall receive from His fulness the treasures of His grace. Faith does not bring Christ to the soul, but brings the soul to Christ. "Say not in thine heart, Who shall ascend into heaven? that is, to bring Christ down from above; or, Who shall descend into the deep? that is, to bring up Christ again from the dead. But what saith it? The word is nigh thee, even in thy mouth, and in thy heart; that is the word of faith which we preach; that if thou shalt confess with thy mouth the Lord Jesus, and shalt believe in thine heart that God hath raised Him from the dead, thou shalt be saved." "Only believe." "All things are possible to him that believeth." Such was the advice of St. Paul to the jailer at Philippi, who asked, "What must I do to be saved?" The Apostle set him about the work of believing. "Believe on the Lord Jesus Christ, and thou shalt be saved." "This is the work of God, that ye believe in Him, whom He hath sent."

The youngest sister in the triad, is Christian *Hope*. We say *Christian* hope, because there are other hopes that influence the mind. There are good hopes and bad hopes, true hopes and false hopes, — hopes laid up on earth that will disappoint the heart, and hopes garnered in heaven that will never fade. The star, that guides the Christian's course through stormy seas, shines from celestial skies. The haven, where he seeks his repose, lies on no earthly coast. It is embowered in no sheltered inlet, by fragrant flowers, and verdant fields, and tropic groves. It is reserved in no sequestered nook, where crystal waves and golden sands invite from sterner climes. The home of the soul is fast by the throne of God, where the waters of perennial life flow gently, and the sun of unclouded day shines steadily. And as the heart is often wearied with fading hopes, and sighs despondingly for rest, the hope inspired by the Gospel, comes like a bright and beautiful bird from the better world, to cheer us amid the darkness. It sings to us its sweetest songs when the spirit is saddest. It wakes its sunniest notes when the soul is harassed, and tightening the slender fibres of our hearts, that grief has torn away, it points beyond the grave and says, " *There* remaineth a rest for the people of God." The eye of Faith and Hope sweeps, at one glance, both sides the dark river of death — takes in at one view, the mortal and immortal scenery — sees on this side, earthly dwellings falling to decay, gathering gloom and flickering sunshine, dark clouds and deep waters, hanging over the landscape ; and on the *other side* descries gloriously, in the distance, the golden towers of the New Jerusalem, the bowers of the heavenly paradise, and the redeemed and glorified in their ecstasies, reposing in the sunlight of the Lamb. Such is the land of its rest, and the home of its promise. The

Christian, as he views this rich, this comprehensive, this splendid and heavenly prospect, in all its fulness, reality, and dignity, is furnished with holy incentives to action, and reckons that the sufferings of this present time are not worthy to be compared with the glory that shall be revealed. He travels toward the scene of his happiness with a mind elastic and buoyant, and finds the yoke of Christ easy, and His burden light. Pushing aside the obstacles that impede his progress, and fixing his steadfast eye on the crown of life, held out to him, to beckon him onward and upward, he aspires towards it, with an energy invincible and resolute, hoping to put his foot upon the neck of every foe, and to wave the victor's palm, — hoping to be glorified with the glory of his triumphant Redeemer, and to outshine the brightness of the sun in his meridian lustre, — hoping to be perfect in every grace, to be free from every sin, to be perfectly holy, and to be perfectly happy, and to be forever with the Lord.

How much the influence of this hope contributes to solace and support the mind, amid the manifold chances and changes of this mortal life, it is almost needless to affirm. It is an anchor of the soul sure and steadfast, entering into that, which is within the veil. Life's sorrows and sufferings may beat like a raging storm upon the spirit; blow after blow may fall on the stricken and bleeding heart; wave piled on wave, like the surging billows of a tempestuous sea, may break over the tossed and troubled soul; but hope in God holds the mind serenely in danger, and disposes it to retain its confidence, which hath " great recompense of reward." You are summoned, it may be, to witness the last moments of endeared connections. Death's hand has severed the fairest flowers of your earthly promise. The curtain drops and darkens your future prospects. But Hope comes soothingly to your aid, in the trying crisis, and whispers words of comfort, about reunion above, where ties that bind us to loved ones are never broken. You stand by the grass-grown sod that covers full half your earthly joys. Your heart is dissolved in grief, and you seem to covet for a while the sleep of the sleeper beneath. You feel as if it would be rest, to slumber, in that silent bed from all your care; but Hope gives forth her voice, and speaks of the Resurrection and the Life, — mortal putting on immortality, and the Saints' sleeping in Jesus, waking up in His likeness. The scene instantly changes; and the coffined clay, and the mouldering dust, are allowed to rest, in the safe-keeping of the Lord, who has promised to " raise it up again at the last day."

Christian hope is therefore more than hope generally. It is hope with all its attractiveness, and with none of its uncertainty, — hope with all the beauty and brilliancy that usually fascinate, and with none of that delusiveness which so often deceives, — hope with a bland and soothing voice, whispering nothing, but truth, — hope with untiring wing, lifting the soul to regions of glory, honor, immortality, eternal life. Christ is its author, Christ its object, Christ its medium, Christ its model and foundation.

"He gives our souls a lively hope
That they shall never die."

Other hopes droop and die, like leaves in Autumn; this puts forth bloom amid the snows of infirmity and age, changing winter into beauty, and dreariness into light and rejoicing.

The most sanguine temperament must acknowledge that human hopes are seldom realized. We may indulge in visions of romance, and bid defiance to the evil day, and form schemes for happiness for years to come. But experience soon undeceives us. We take but a few steps in life without finding the world to be a turbulent scene. Changes perpetually await us, and we feel the thorns of the wilderness, in which we dwell. Our most cherished hopes are frequently blasted in the bud; our designs defeated at the very moment of execution, and we meet with sorrow, vexation, and disappointment on every hand. Just when we have laid a plan for a happy life, when we have found out a few chosen friends, and have begun to enjoy that little circle, in which we would wish to live, and to die, a stroke unexpected overthrows our hopes, and lays our schemes in the dust. When after much labor and care we have fondly succeeded in raising the goodly structure, and fenced it in, as we imagine, from every storm that blows, an invisible hand interposes, and brings it to naught.

There is no stability, but in that sure and steadfast hope, which takes a loftier range, and fastens on objects, which the limits of earth and time are unable to disturb. The good hope through grace never disappoints. The man who enjoys it cannot but be happy. He may be poor in the estimation of the world, and have to contend with difficulties, many and various, but with the means of grace, and the hope of glory, he has heaven in his heart; and the God of hope so fills him with "joy and peace in believing, that he abounds in hope, through the power of the Holy Ghost."

The queen grace of the cluster is CHARITY. Her holiest and divinest name is Love. She is so called in several portions of the New Testament. It is said of her, "Love is the fulfilling of the law;" "Faith, which worketh by love." Love among the other virtues is, as poets have expressed it, Gabriel among archangels, a seraph loftier than the seraph train. The Apostle, commenting on the group, ascribes a distinction to Charity, which belongs not to the others. "And now abideth faith, hope, charity, these three, but the greatest of these is charity." The preëminence, which Charity holds over the other sisters, excites no jealousy, and impairs in no way the connection that subsists between them. Separate from them, she can have no existence. Any attempt to dispense with *their* coöperation would be like endeavoring to raise a superstructure without a foundation. We are accordingly exhorted to give all diligence to add to our faith virtue, and to virtue brotherly kindness, and to brotherly kindness charity.

Charity is the greatest in rank. She is what may be called an ultimate virtue, while Faith and Hope are merely preliminaries,— the instrumental means of bringing her into exercise. "For the end of the commandment is *love* out of a pure heart, and of a good conscience, and of faith unfeigned."

Charity is the greatest in resemblance. She

is like God, for God is love. The impress of His likeness on the heart is the highest glory of created beings. It is the richest gem in the crown of honor. It is heaven-like and glorious, the element of the just made perfect, and of angels in light.

Charity is the greatest in utility. We believe and hope with an immediate reference to ourselves; but love is a social feeling, and sheds its influence on others. Through the aid of faith and hope we were made heirs of salvation, ministered to by angels; and love qualifies us to act the part of ministering angels in our turn. The welling up of the heart's affection to God will most certainly develop the feature of love to man,—love limited to no circle, restricted by no partialities, around which no boundary line is drawn by prejudice or aversion, and which realizes as its proper objects, friends, foes, and strangers.

The grace of Charity is preëminently the greatest in duration. She will ascend with us to the skies, and live in our souls forever. We have no reason to suppose that Faith, in any modification of the term, will be necessary in heaven. The objects to which she now refers are absent, but *there*, they will be present in all their nearness. Nor is there any just ground to conclude that Hope will have existence in the heavenly state. But the flame of holy love will burn in every bosom, sparkle in every eye, and inspire every tongue.

We take leave of Faith and Hope at the gate of death. Were it possible we could drop a tear as we enter the mansions of our Father's house above, it would be at bidding an everlasting farewell to these beloved and profitable companions. They have been our solace at every stage of our heavenward journey. They are our staff and support in the dark valley. They give us victory over all our adversaries, and are our ceaseless privilege and joy.

Now glance at these sisters separately. Observe their attitude, countenances, and the features of divinity which they so finely develop. Look at the firm step, the majestic gait, the fixed yet serene gaze of Faith. See how she tramples upon thrones, and dominions, and principalities, and powers, and all the paraphernalia of emblazoned rank and titled dignity,— how she spurns the pomps and pleasures of this passing world, and courts joys which cannot decay,— how closely she walks with God, and holds fellowship with the kingly Mediator,— how steadfastly she looks into the open heavens, beholding with open face the glory of the Lord, catching the Saviour's reflected likeness, and exhibiting His image.

Look at the younger sister, Hope, — her countenance radiant with light, her form ethereal, her movements vivid and elastic, obstacles receding at her approach, before her all brightness, her finger pointing to visions of beauty and blessedness beyond the shadows of the sepulchre. Thither the warm current of her desires and emotions flow, and thence is all her expectation.

And look at the lovely Charity, the friend and almoner of our race. See her penetrating the abodes of sorrow, mitigating want and wretchedness, hushing the groans of creation, and healing the woes of humanity. Survey her splendid operations and achievements within the hallowed pale of Christianity, — the institutions she has formed, the heathen countries she has visited, the dark places of the earth she has enlightened, and the multitude of the outcast and perishing she has brought to the foot of the cross. Reflect on her sublime combination of energy, property, and influence, and ask, What are these but monuments of that heaven-born "charity," which "suffereth long and is kind," — "charity" which "envieth not, vaunteth not itself, is not puffed up, doth not behave itself unseemly, seeketh not her own, is not easily provoked, thinketh no evil, rejoiceth not in iniquity, but rejoiceth in the truth, beareth all things, believeth all things, hopeth all things, endureth all things?"

The exercise of charity constitutes one of the chief springs of happiness, which God has so mercifully pointed out to man. It flows most beautifully and effectively where there is most good to be done. When a rose-tree puts out its buds, and the air is soft, and the sky genial, it is not long before they burst. The life within is so abundant that it is unable to contain itself. It must needs go forth and gladden the air with blossomed brightness, and swimming fragrance. If, when thus ripe, it refused to expand, it would rot at the core and die. Now Christian charity is just its counterpart; it is godliness with its petals spread, developing itself, and making the earth a happier world. It is true blessedness, the life of God in the soul, diffusing itself in kindly emotions and good offices. As we are moved by its impulse we shall do good unto all men, especially unto those who are of the household of faith. We admire the grace and beauty of the triple crown, and must exemplify it as our own. " Without faith it is impossible to please God." " Without hope we are of all men the most miserable." And " though we speak with the tongue of men, and of angels, and have not charity, we become as sounding brass or a tinkling cymbal."

The superlative importance of this triplet makes it the first prayer of the Church for her members that they " may be steadfast in faith, joyful through hope, and rooted in charity."

The culture of the graces is sought at the very threshold of our Christian life, in every festival and fast, to the last, and at the last, when having "served our generation according to the will of God," we are gathered to our fathers, in the confidence of a certain faith; in the comfort of a reasonable, religious, and holy hope," in favor with God, "and in perfect charity with the world."

## THE THREE JEWISH FESTIVALS.

THREE times a year all the Jewish males were required to go up to Jerusalem to celebrate certain festivals, and to make an offering unto the Lord. And "thither the tribes went up, the tribes of the Lord, unto the testimony of Israel, to give thanks unto the name of the Lord." One might suppose that the enforcement of such a law would leave their wives and children, and property, unprotected and exposed to the invading foe. But God condescended to assure them that He would so influence the hearts of their adversaries that none should covet their possessions, and none should harm them. The object of the arrangement was to extract a continued proof of their confidence in God's protection, and to secure the unity of their several tribes. As in the coming dispensation there was to be "one Lord, one faith, one baptism, and one God and Father of all," so they were to have one chosen place where the adorable Jehovah should be inquired of by His worshippers, one altar on which the sacrifices might bleed acceptably, and one censer from which the incense might rise uninterruptedly to His throne, and secure His favor. Nothing certainly could tend more admirably to cement them together in one common brotherhood than this constant communion in sacred things. It impressed them afresh with a sense of the common mercies which their nation had experienced, and of the common privileges in which they rejoiced. With the same victims to offer, the same pardon to implore, the same goodness to be grateful for, and the same hope of a glorious Messiah to rejoice in, they had no separate interest or private object to distract them in their united worship. "Jerusalem was" a city that was "at unity in itself"; and the several tribes repaired to it as one man to bow before the Lord, and to tender Him the offering and oblation which He had graciously appointed.

The SPRING FESTIVAL of the chosen people was the Passover, or Feast of unleavened bread. This was the historic truth of their deliverance from the destroying angel, when the first-born of Egypt were smitten. As a festive memorial of that eventful night, which served to introduce them into an independent and separate existence, they were accustomed to greet its annual occurrence with thanksgiving and praise. The institution was the more remarkable because it dated the commencement of their ecclesiastical year. The month in which they were thrust out of Egypt was ordained to be the first month. On the fourteenth day of the month, the day of the full moon, between the sun's decline and his setting, they were to kill the paschal lamb, which was to be a male of a year old, free from disease and blemish. And as each house had its own special deliverance, so in each there was to be a domestic celebration. If the household were too small to consume the lamb at one meal, two or more families were at liberty to unite on the occasion. But no part of the lamb was to be left until the morning. It was necessary perhaps to give this precaution, to prevent its being applied to superstitious uses. Besides, what was left would be very soon subject to corruption, and it would not be seemly that what had been offered to the Lord should be exposed to decay. If any portion of it therefore remained, it was to be consumed by fire. With the blood of the slaughtered victim they sprinkled the door-posts and lintels of their houses, that the angel of death, at the sight of the blood, might pass over and spare, and leave in safety the dwellings so marked. Accordingly, wherever the angel saw the blood thus applied he reverently retired. The arm of the Almighty fell with crushing calamity through the length and breadth of the land. The Egyptians sought to brave the terrible threat, that had been uttered, by hilarity and mirth. Mansions were brilliantly lit. Sounds of gladness and revelry echoed through their spacious halls. Sweet voices sang to the soft strains of the Egyptian harp, the minstrelsy of Thebes. But it was the night of the Lord. The angel spread his wings o'er the blast; and there was a cry of horror and dismay. The first-born of every family was stricken. The eldest of his father's house was touched by an invisible hand, and laid a corpse. The gladness was instantly changed into mourning, and the shouts of merriment into anguish and wailing. The marriage procession was arrested in the midst of its glee. The cry heard at midnight, "Behold the bridegroom cometh," was suddenly hushed. The looked-for home was thrown into wild confusion. The bridegroom was smitten by a power unseen in the midst of his joy. The whole land was aroused into commotion. The destroyer had trodden alike the floor of the cottage and the hall of the palace. The prince found no safety in his power, nor the peasant in his obscurity. The first-born of Pharoah, who sat on his throne, and the first-born of the captive that was in the dungeon; and all the first-born of cattle were smitten. There was a great cry throughout all the land of Egypt. The king's heart smote him with trembling; and he sent for Moses and Aaron, whom he had forbidden to see his face again, and urged them to depart with the people with all possible speed. "Take your flocks, and herds," said he, "and be gone." The people were more anxious than their sovereign to hasten their departure, and gave them jewels of gold, and jewels of silver, and such other things as they asked, to get rid of such troublesome bondmen.

The arrangement of the Exodus discovered an interposition on the part of God, which the Passover as a commemorative institution was designed to keep fresh in the mind. The rites and usages of that solemn feast were so peculiar, and made so marked an inroad upon the ordinary customs of social life, that it was adapted by its very nature to be an enduring memorial of that eventful night. We believe it is mainly owing to this ancient festival that the Hebrew nation has in all ages retained such a vivid conception of its remarkable deliverance.

The Passover was observed with preparations symbolical of haste. They partook of it in the posture and equipment of travellers.

Their outward robes, that were usually free and flowing, were drawn up closely around the body into a girdle, to leave its action unfettered and easy. Their loins were girded; their shoes on their feet; and they ate the sacred meal *standing*, staff in hand. The flesh of the lamb was roasted, not boiled, for the reason probably that it occupied less time. It was eaten with unleavened bread, as being also expressive of haste. They were on the eve of leaving Egypt, and it may have been partly to remind them of the speed with which they took their departure, that unleavened bread formed a part of the commemoration.

The Passover was typical in its import of our redemption by Christ. The paschal lamb was emblematic of the Lamb of God that taketh away the sin of the world. The blood that streamed on Jewish altars pointed specifically to the blood of Christ, that cleanseth us from all sin. The long series of sacrifices had reference to Christ, our passover, sacrificed for us. The Good-Friday of His crucifixion witnessed a "full, perfect, and sufficient sacrifice, oblation, and satisfaction for the sins of the whole world." We may have our doubts and misgivings of any personal interest in the benefits of the atonement, and many a freezing cloud may cast its cold shadow upon our hearts; but the blood of Christ has been shed. The offering, once for all, has been made and accepted; and our hearts need not be troubled, if we believe in God, and believe also in Jesus.

On the night of His betrayal, our blessed Lord merged the feast of the Passover into the solemn sacrament of His own supper. He came not to destroy the law and the prophets, but to fulfil; not to abrogate ancient rites, but to exalt them from a typical shadow to a real substance. As the blossoms of spring fade and pass into the fruits of autumn, so the types and shadows of the old dispensation were ordained to be realized, in all their sweetness, under the economy of the Spirit. Mark the attitude of the Saviour in the large upper room in Jerusalem. The festive board was spread. The Master and the servants sat down. And Jesus said, "With desire I have desired to eat this passover with you before I suffer." What a glimpse it gives us into the sanctuary of His inmost soul! What solicitude for the circle of His friends! What a closing up of the series of fourteen hundred passovers by the sacrifice of Himself! The Passover being eaten, "Jesus took bread, and blessed it and brake it, and gave it to His disciples," with these emphatic words, "Take, eat, this is my body which is given for you. Do this in remembrance of me. Likewise, after supper, He took the cup, and when He had given thanks He gave it to them saying, Drink ye all of it: this cup is the new testament in my blood, which is shed for you and for many for the remission of sins." The blessed Jesus thus bequeaths to us the incomparable legacy of His body and blood; the fruit of His atoning life, sufferings, and death. "Wherefore," according to His holy institution, we cheerfully celebrate, before His divine Majesty, the festive memorial, which He has commanded us to observe, " having in remembrance His blessed passion and precious death, His mighty resurrection and glorious ascension, rendering unto Him most hearty thanks for the innumerable benefits procured unto us by the same." The supper of the Lord is the picture of our best friend dying to save us; lays open to our view His broken body, and pierced side, and flowing blood; reflects the shadow of the cross, and the splendor of the crown, and tells of wrath that has passed away, of sunshine that gilds the valley where we are sojourners, and that sprinkles with bright beams the everlasting hills, beyond which is our home, and our heart, and our treasure.

The SUMMER FESTIVAL of the Jews was the Pentecost, so called from a Greek word which signifies fifty; because it commenced on the fiftieth day after the Passover. It commemorated, moreover, the giving of the Law from Mount Sinai, on the fiftieth day after they left Egypt. The Hebrews call it the "Feast of Weeks," on account of its being held just seven weeks from the paschal feast. During the interim of the two festivals they were supposed to be actively engaged in the labors of the harvest, so as to be ready at the holy convocation, to render thanksgiving to Almighty God for the bounties of His hand. The obligation to observe it sabbatically was not peculiar to this any more than to the others. Its distinction lay in its occasion and purport, and in the solemn presentation of the first-fruits of the wheat harvest to the Lord.

At every recurrence of the season the Jews began to rally by common consent within the limits of their several districts. They mustered at the principal cities, to go up to Jerusalem, as to a common centre. They set out on their journey, preceded by a bullock intended for the sacrifice, his horns gilded, and his head decorated with a garland of olive branches. The people encouraged each other with expressions of enthusiasm, as, " I was glad when they said unto me, Let us go into the house of the Lord. Our feet shall stand within thy gates, O Jerusalem." This was particularly their language as they drew near the city. On entering the metropolis they chanted, " Jerusalem is builded as a city that is compact together, whither the tribes go up, the tribes of the Lord unto the testimony of Israel, to give thanks unto the name of the Lord; for there are set thrones of judgment, the thrones of the house of David." The residents, thronging their doorways and housetops to greet them, bid them pray for the peace of Jerusalem; and the tribes replied, "They shall prosper that love thee. Peace be within thy walls, and prosperity within thy palaces. For my brethren and companions' sake, I will now say, Peace be within thee. Because of the house of the Lord our God, I will seek thy good." The procession moved on to the foot of the mountain, on which the Temple stood, repeating as they ascended, in tones of impressive and melodious accents, "Praise ye the Lord." And they sang in the Temple the thirtieth Psalm, worshipping according to their ritual.

"When the day of Pentecost was fully come, and they were all with one accord in one place," there came "suddenly a sound from heaven, as of a rushing, mighty wind," and filled the house where they were sitting. And there appeared forked flames of fire, as when the lightnings flash, and the sky is ablaze, and rested upon the disciples. "And they were all filled with the Holy Ghost; and began to speak with other tongues as the Spirit gave them utterance." One would stand up in that vast assembly and pour forth, in strains of inspired eloquence, the most profound views of the divine economy. Another would explain the mystery of truths that had been concealed for ages under the Jewish dispensation. A third would discourse with fluency on the sublimities of the Gospel. And a fourth, officiating in the capacity of an interpreter, would render all that had been spoken into the vernacular language of the people. The intellectual phenomenon was the Lord's doing. The promised Spirit had descended. The Comforter had come.

The infant Church was so replenished with divine strength, that it seemed all at once to attain to the growth and vigor of manhood. The vineyard of the Lord was refreshed and beautified. The trees of righteousness put forth fresh shoots, fresh verdure, and more abundant fruit. The word was clothed with fresh power. New territories were added to the domains of the Church. New tracts of the moral wilderness were taken into the Lord's garden. The whole multitude that believed were of one heart and of one mind. Oh! it was such a scene as earth saw never, — such as heaven stooped down to see.

The descent of the Spirit attested the reality of the ascension, and of the truths and hopes which it acknowledges and inspires. It was the Lord's ascension gift, rich and munificent, with which He signalized and graced His accession to the mediatorial throne. If He had collected all the treasures of earth, and multiplied them a thousand-fold, and poured them out at the feet of His people, they would have been utterly inadequate to the greatness of the occasion. The unconfined benevolence of the Saviour's heart impelled Him to give something worthy of Himself, and that He might give all gifts in one, He gave the Holy, Sanctifying, Saving Spirit.

The Spirit came to inaugurate a new era,

and make our hearts His home; came to bear witness to Christ; to take of the things of Christ, and reveal them to us; came to act as Christ's vicegerent on earth; to fix the eye of our minds on Christ; to stir up our dead consciences, to assist our endeavors to be holy, to quicken our sensibility, to make our bodies His temple, our souls His empire, and to "renew us more and more, till we come to His heavenly kingdom." To the Spirit we are indebted for every conquest we achieve over our spiritual adversaries, and for every step we take, in our heavenward path. Whatever is lovely in the Church is the product of His quickening influence. "It is the Spirit that quickeneth." If there are fruits and flowers that gladden us, we can look up to Him with the acknowledgment, "These be Thy works, Parent of good." Only let the quickening and germinating influences of the Spirit be more ardently sought and obtained, and like a genial thaw in spring, there will be a melting away of unhallowed prejudices; there will be an expansion of generous sympathies;

there will be a budding forth of precious graces and productions, unfolding a beauty and perfume, like the smell of a field which the Lord hath blessed. Inward impulses will spring up into outward manifestations. The heart will touch the lip and transform the life ; and the seeds of divine grace will appear green on the surface, growing in all the luxuriance of a spiritual vegetation. Child of God, born anew of water and of the Spirit, cherish toward the loving Spirit the respect and adoration that you would wish to show to the Saviour, if He dwelt corporeally among you. "Be filled with the Spirit." "Walk in the Spirit." "Live in the Spirit." "Mind the things of the Spirit." "Grieve not the Holy Spirit of God, by whom you are sealed unto the day of redemption."

The Autumnal Festival was the Feast of Tabernacles. This was celebrated at the close of the agricultural year, and was called the Feast of Ingathering at the year's end. The ceremonies continued eight days, the first and last of which were the most solemn. "On the last day, that great day of the feast, Jesus stood and cried, "If any man thirst, let him come unto Me and drink." The special object of the feast was to celebrate the goodness of God, that protected their fathers in the wilderness, when they dwelt in tents and booths. The Jews cut down branches of palm-trees, and willows, and dwelt under tents eight days, in memory of their ancestors, who dwelt in tents forty years in the desert.

The intention of the arrangement was to remind them that they were "strangers and pilgrims on the earth," travellers to a "better country, that is a heavenly." The present world was never intended to be our home; only as preparatory to a higher and nobler state of being. "This is not our rest, because it is polluted." "Here we have no continuing city." The props of life are broken down one after another. Changes and war are against us. The enemy scatters thickly around his fiery darts. Stars fall. Flowers fade. Friends die. The rose loses its fragrance. The oak of the mountain drops its leaves. The mountains themselves decay. The ocean ebbs and flows, and will one day roll its last billow to the shore. The sun shines only for a season, and will some night set in darkness, heedless of the voice of the morning. The life of man, compared with inanimate objects, is even more ephemeral. His duration is a swift decay. "He fleeth as a shadow and continueth not." There is no stopping-place between the cradle and the tomb. We hurry through the world, and leave everything behind us. We throw a passing glance on enamelled meads, and purling brooks, and whatever else may chance to charm and allure us. We feel a pleasure in the contemplation of these scenes; but before we can analyze the objects of our enjoyment we have lost sight of them forever. To beautiful prospects and a smiling country, rocks, ravines, and precipices, and rugged paths often succeed. These things annoy and afflict us for the moment, and the next we are beyond their reach.

Were it not that we are home-bound pilgrims, nearing the mansions of our "Father's house," the thought of our fleeting existence would be apt to produce pensiveness, and to throw over life's arena a tinge of melancholy. But we are journeying unto the place of which the Lord hath said, "I will surely give it you." Sometimes our progress is considerable; at other times slender, and at all times less than we could wish. There are occasions when we are cheered with hope, and gladdened with success, and anon discouraged by disquietudes and disappointments, and the "difficulties of the way." But the characteristics of a pilgrimage are endurance, and perseverance. The fare may be hard, and the dangers great, but we have a glorious convoy, and a heavenly guide. The circumstances of the journey are all provided for with infinite wisdom. If the sun shines smilingly, we have cause to rejoice. If the sky be tempestuous, it is of little moment, we are only pilgrims. The way is a right one to the city of habitation.

At neither of the three festivals were the Jews to appear before the Lord empty. There was to be an open-hearted liberality at each of them. Every man was to give as he was able, according to the blessing of the Lord, his God, which He had given him. To whom much was given, of them much was required; and such as had received freely, were to give freely. It is hardly possible to impoverish one's self by giving to the Lord. The danger lies in withholding more than is meet, and it tendeth to poverty. There are those "who profess and call themselves Christians," who will contribute to the cause of Christ, when they can do so without *feeling* it. The blessed Jesus *felt* all that He did for us, and deemed the purchase not too costly to buy us with His blood. The genius of the Gospel is liberality. It is essentially eucharistical. Its glad tidings awaken glad feelings that express themselves in cheerful sacrifices and thankful offerings. "The Lord loveth a cheerful giver;" and none of His people need ever lack that grateful motive, which makes a cheerful gift. Think of the Bible, the Church, the Saviour, the Comforter, the means of grace, and the hope of glory; and casting your mite into the treasury, say, "Thanks be unto God for His unspeakable gift.

# THE THREE SACRED MOUNTAINS.

THE mountains Sinai, Tabor, and Calvary were made to sustain an intimate connection with each other in the plan of human redemption. They were identified with all that was great and glorious in the interests of our race. The rays of ineffable majesty, which shone so luminously on the one, darted horizontally to the other in softened splendor, and thence to the third, as unfolding the unveiled glory and eloquence of Heaven. The events of each were so many links of the same chain, connecting a group, of which it might be said, — "There the Lord commanded the blessing, even life for evermore."

To the rugged mountain of Sinai, which afterwards became so signal in the history of the chosen people, they had come in their wanderings from a land, where for several generations they had been bond-servants to the Pharaohs. The hum and buzz of that mighty nation, favored of God, was heard at its base. Their tents lay scattered like snow-flakes, and they were in waiting expectation of fresh instructions before proceeding farther. While tarrying in this position, a dark thunder-cloud came drifting along the sky, in the direction of Sinai. The people looked up to it with fear and trembling, when lo! the thunder began to roll from its depths, and the lightnings to flash. That cloud was God's pavilion. The Lord hath His way in the whirlwind, and in the storm, and the clouds are the dust of His feet. The commotion, which it created, caused the mountain to quiver to its centre. "God came from Teman, and the Holy One from Mount Paran; from His right hand went a fiery law." "The mountains melted from before the Lord, even that Sinai, from before the Lord God of Israel." The thunderings, and lightnings, and thick darkness were as if the pent up elements of some terrible volcano were being quickly discharged. "And the smoke thereof ascended as the smoke of a great furnace, and the whole mount quaked greatly.

Amid convulsions so tremendous, the shrill blast of a trumpet was heard. "And when the voice of the trumpet sounded long, and waxed louder and louder, Moses spake, and God answered him by a voice." It was a voice of solemn majesty, addressed specifically to the Jewish lawgiver, requiring him to ascend the mountain, where the cloud received him into its bosom, and concealed him from the curious gaze of the multitude below. The High and Lofty One deigned to converse with him there, as a man converseth with his friend. The Creator and the creature met in hallowed communion. "And the Lord said unto Moses, Go down, set bounds about the mount, and sanctify it, and charge the people lest they brake through unto the Lord to gaze, and many of them perish." And the Lord proclaimed, in the audience of the assembled concourse, "I am the Lord, thy God, which brought thee out of the land of Egypt, out of the house of bondage. Thou shalt have no other gods before me." The decalogue was delivered with august and thrilling sanctions, causing the hearts of the people to dissolve in fear, and Nature to stand awe-stricken, and adoring before it. " And all the people when they saw the thunderings, and the lightnings, and the noise of the trumpet, and the mountain smoking, removed and stood afar off; and they said unto Moses, Speak thou with us, and we will hear: but let not God speak with us, lest we die."

When the fearful roar was hushed, and the last echo of the trumpet had died away, the silence was only broken by the accents of the Eternal, inviting Moses once more into the Mount, to receive the tables of the law, to bind and govern them, and their descendants forever. " The tables were of stone, written on both their sides: on the one side, and on the other side were they written. And the tables were the work of God, and the writing was the writing of God, graven on the tables."

The scene that followed was one of insufferable splendor. The stars of night were extinguished by its dazzling brilliancy, and the moon was eclipsed by its glory. Never had the wondering eyes of man rested on so striking a phenomenon. "The sight of the glory of the Lord was like a devouring fire on the top of the mountain, in the eyes of the children of Israel."

Where now was the leader of their tribes? He was somewhere in that brightness, holding converse with the ineffable Jehovah. Forty days and forty nights he was privileged to breathe that serener atmosphere, and acquired, by supernatural manifestations, what would eminently qualify him for his task in the wilderness. As during that period no tidings had been received of him, the people lapsed into idleness, and from idleness into pleasure, and from pleasure into idolatry, and said unto Aaron, "Up, make us gods which shall go before us; for as for this Moses, the man that brought us up out of the land of Egypt, we wot not what is become of him." This was their proposal while the most extraordinary revelations of Heaven were yet fresh in their memories. And they made a golden calf, and danced around it in boisterous revelry. When Moses was descending the Mount, bearing in his arms the tables of the law, and had come within hearing of the camp, Joshua said, "There is a noise of war in the camp;" and as they drew near and saw the idolatrous worship, the anger of Moses was kindled, and he cast the tables of the covenant out of his hands, and brake them beneath the Mount, in the presence of the people. He then took the golden calf, which they had made, and burned it in the fire, and ground it to powder, and mixed it with water, and made the children of Israel drink of it. And he commanded the Levites to take every man his sword, and slay every man his brother, and every man his companion, and every man his neighbor, showing neither favor nor affection. And there fell of the people that day about three thousand men. The Lord also sent a grievous plague among them, and refused to accompany them any farther on their journey to Canaan, and threatened to disinherit them. The refusal and the threat fell upon their fears like the shock of an earthquake, and they "took off their ornaments and wept."

At this critical juncture, the heroic commander of Israel was requested to turn aside into the tabernacle, for renewed intercourse with the Almighty. While he tarried there, the people of his charge were the subjects of torturing suspense, lest he should return and inform them that the Majesty of heaven and earth was inflexible in His decision to cast them off. But having improved the opportunity by importunate intercession on their behalf, he so far succeeded, that the Lord intimated His intention of sending an angel to conduct them. But no angel,— no, not all the angels in heaven, could fill up the place of departed Deity. The Hebrew Legislator therefore continued his entreaty that the Lord would be favorable yet once more, and vouchsafe to reveal Himself as the guide of their way. The fervent petition was granted. The Lord said, "My presence shall go with thee, and I will give thee peace."

The province of prayer is to enlarge our desires the more they are gratified; so the prophet now determined to ask for a personal favor, and with holy reverence said, "I beseech thee, show me thy glory." He had already seen some splendid manifestations of it, but he felt as though every fresh development only increased his desire for another. Hence he was anxious for an additional exhibition of it, especially for himself. The request was responded to in a manner, that was both novel and unexpected. "Behold, there is a place by me," said God, "and thou shalt stand upon a rock: and it shall come to pass, while my glory passeth by, that I will put thee in a cleft of the rock; and will cover thee with my hand while I pass by: and I will take away mine hand, and thou shalt see my back parts: but my face shall not be seen." And what was the result? Did the rock rend asunder at the presence of the Lord? Did the God of the universe display the greatness of His power? Did Moses strain his expectant eye to pierce the covering of the Almighty? The Lord passed by him in a cloud, dark and impenetrable, and proclaimed the "name of the Lord, merciful and gracious, long-suffering and abundant in goodness and truth, keeping mercy for thousands, forgiving iniquity, transgression, and sin." This was precisely the manifestation that he needed at the time, and which God alone was capable of affording. Just as the sun can only be seen by his own shining, so the ever adorable Jehovah can only be known by His own revealing. Would we see the glory of God, we must look for it in Christ. "He is the brightness of the Father's glory, and the express image of His person." There is in Him the glory of wisdom, and knowledge, and grace, and every attribute, in absolute perfection.

The tables of the law, that were broken, Moses was commanded to replace, by hewing out two tables of stone like them; and the Lord condescended to write with His finger, once more, the Ten Commandments. The code is presented us in the small compass of a few short lines, in the twentieth chapter of Exodus. It is more just and comprehensive, more suited to the condition of men, and better fitted to promote their happiness, than any other that has ever been promulgated. It is perfection itself. We can detect no fault in it, — cannot add to it, — cannot take from it without detracting from its value; "for the end of the commandment is charity, out of a pure heart, and of a good conscinece, and of faith unfeigned." Said the Apostle, " The law is our schoolmaster to bring us to Christ." " I had not known sin, but by the law." " By the law is the knowledge of sin." The law is a rule by which to distinguish right from wrong, good from evil, truth from error. And as the straightness of the rule detects the crookedness of the workmanship, so the law of God exposes our deficiencies, and shows how far we have fallen short of His glory. The resemblance of it is to God Himself. It is a transcript of His perfections, an exhibition of His character and glorious attributes. As the voice of the Almighty, it speaks directly to the soul, giving utterance and energy to the enlightened dictates of the man within. Like the elemental fire, it is not only present where it is grossly visible, but all pervading. Its gaze is fixed with lidless and unslumbering eye on all the thoughts and ways of this apostate world. It beholds nothing of an indifferent nature in the whole scene; but notes, weighs, and discriminates whatever transpires, discovering everywhere, and in everything, the elements of approval, or, condemnation. Opening up the dark and secret chambers of the heart, it shows what sins are lurking there, that have not ventured to come forth into action, — evil in its rudiment, rage in the spark, licentiousness in the glance, and murder ambushed in unbreathed and unsuspected thought.

To the thoughts of the heart the law reaches with the nicest accuracy, throwing over them the bridle of restraint, and aiming to bring them in subjection to the authority of Christ. The obedience which it requires is perfect, constant, and universal, — obedience at all times, on the part of all men, and in all things, — uniform, unbroken obedience, from the first dawn of moral accountability till our life's end. No allowance is made for human infirmity, — no assistance offered to human frailty. The whole current of existence must be uninterrupted by a single insurgent feeling, uncontaminated by a single spot, and unrelaxing in a single purpose. All the powers of the intellect, all the capabilities of the moral feeling, and all the ardor and intensity of the awakened affection must be fixed and concentrated on God. Such is the beautiful standard which the law has set up. Do this and live, is its language. Do it without exception, — do it cheerfully; " for he who offends in one point is guilty of all."

Before the bar of God's righteous judgment the whole world is found guilty. " There is none righteous, no not one." The law condemns us. How then can a man be just with God? This is a question of vast and momentous importance, — a question which all the learning of the wise, and all the understanding of the prudent, could not answer apart from the Gospel. The scenes on Tabor and Calvary answer it most effectually. They declare that we are "justified freely by His grace, through the redemption that is in Christ Jesus." " Christ is the end of the law for righteousness to every one that believeth." " By Him all that believe are justified freely from all things, from which they could not be justified by the law of Moses." The Son of God has magnified the law and made it honorable, — submitted to its penal sanctions; satisfied perfectly its demands; and though His sacrifice does not release us from the restraints of the Divine government, yet "the spirit of life in Christ Jesus frees us from the law of sin and death." The moral law is still obligatory upon us, in all its force. Its principles are found in accordance with our interest and happiness, and have their home in the inmost depths of the pure in heart.

Sinai and Horeb are different parts of the same mountain. The shadow of the former falls on the latter, and the events ascribed to one are sometimes assigned to the other. They exist together in brotherhood, and should not be severed in the contemplation of God's revelations. From this mountain scenery the murmuring Israelites were miraculously supplied with water. "Moses cried unto the Lord, saying, What shall I do unto this people? they be almost ready to stone me. And the Lord said, Take thy rod wherewith thou smotest the river, and behold I will stand before thee upon the rock in Horeb; and thou shalt smite the rock, and there shall come water out of it, that the people may drink. And Moses did so, in the sight of the elders of Israel." Instantly there was a change of thought and feeling, elasticity of movement, mighty operation, — the turning of the shadow of death into the joy of the morning. Bright scenes appeared through all the tribes. Thousands and tens of thousands press close to the fissures of the rock, to catch the enlivening draught. Thousands and tens of thousands fall down upon their knees to drink of the bubbling flow. Fathers and mothers haste to impart it to their children. Young men and maidens bear it to the lame, the sick, and the dying. All exult in the copiousness of the effusions, and drink abundantly. Next come the cattle in hasty procession,— the oxen, the asses, the sheep, and the goats. The feathered tribes also scent the water, and drink to satiety. It was a glorious sight, causing " the lame to leap as a hart, and the tongue of the dumb to sing." " I will open rivers," says God, " in high places, and fountains in the midst of the valleys. I will make the wilderness a pool of water, and the dry land water-springs. The beasts of the field shall honor me, the dragon and the owl; because I give water in the wilderness, and rivers in the desert, to give drink to my people, my chosen."

The consecration of Sinai, by the presence of Deity, caused it to merit the appellation, "Mount of God." The prophet Elijah, pursued by Jezebel, fled hither for his life. He had betaken himself into the wilderness of Judea, and lay under a juniper-tree, requesting that he might die. The angel of the Lord touched him, and bade him arise, and go to Mount Horeb. He arose, and did eat and drink, and went in the strength of that meat forty days and forty nights. The desert over which he travelled was the same through which the Israelites passed, in the forty years of their wanderings. It was hallowed ground, rich in thoughtful association, and holy memories. The towering heights of Sinai and Horeb were retreats where God was wont to reveal Himself to Moses; and Elijah might suppose that God was about to meet with him, in all the glory of His benignity. The situation in which he found himself in Horeb was one of indescribable solitude; and having crept into a gloomy cave, and wrapped his mantle around him, and laid down to pass the night, the word of the Lord came to him, saying, " What doest thou here, Elijah? And he said, I have been very jealous for the Lord of Hosts, for the children of Israel have forsaken thy covenant, thrown down thy altars, and slain thy prophets with the sword: and I, even I only am left, and they seek my life." And He said, " Go forth and stand upon the Mount before the Lord." And the Lord passed by him in a strong wind, that rent the rocks asunder. The clouds appeared like squadrons of combatants, rushing to conflict. The sands of the desert were agitated like the waves of the sea; and Sinai rocked, as if the terrors of the law-giving were renewed. The commotion produced on the soul of Elijah an overpowering impression of God's awful majesty,—a sentiment of distressing distance; " but the Lord was not in the wind."

The terrors of an earthquake next ensued. The foundations of the hills shook, and were removed. Hills sank and valleys rose. Chasms yawned, and horrible depths discovered themselves. The ruins of Nature surrounded him, causing him to feel the glory of that divine majesty which "looketh upon the earth, and it trembleth."

When the ruffled frame of Nature was calmed, an awful fire passed by, changing the shades of night into the light of day. The mountain was suddenly in a blaze; "but the Lord was not in the fire."

And after the fire, there followed a still small voice,—a soothing undertone,—a gentle whisper. "And it was so, when Elijah heard it, that he wrapped his face in his mantle, and went forth and stood at the entrance of the cave." The accents of love and mercy, which now fell so sweetly upon his ear, had a melting, softening influence, which the kindness and love of God so beautifully effect.

The leaves of time showed the continuation of the same series of Divine manifestations on the summit of Tabor. The terrible things in righteousness, that transpired on Sinai, were ratified on the Mount of Transfiguration, in subdued and softened splendor. The august and glorious Jehovah, who called Moses to the mountain-top in Arabia Petrea, had become the meek and lowly Jesus, who took Peter, James, and John, to a high mountain in Galilee. The drapery of His humiliation was unable to conceal longer the indwelling brightness of the Godhead. The rays of the Shekinah, which had slumbered within, now darted forth, from beneath the enshrouding cloud, with an effulgence that was perfectly overwhelming. The splendor of the Deity pierced through His humanity, beamed in His countenance, and surrounded His whole person with the most dazzling lustre. The glory that had dwelt in Him from eternity, burst forth, in richest radiance. It was not shed upon Him externally, but existed in Him as a portion of that fulness, which dwelt, as in a focus, behind the curtain of the servant's form. "His face shone as the sun, and His raiment was white as the light." It was one of those special occasions, when meekness gave way to majesty, sadness to overpowering gladness, and the look of pity to the grandeur of a God. The gazing disciples were struck with admiration. They could scarcely give credit to their eyes. They could hardly believe that shining One was their Master, with whom they toiled up the wearisome ascent. The discovery of His inner glory was a transporting reflection of pure kindness and love. Its intention was to improve the Apostles in knowledge and grace; to convince them who He really was; to assure them that His government was spiritual; that triumph would certainly succeed and reward His sufferings, and that all His servants will ultimately be glorified with Him.

Wonder now followed wonder in rapid succession. An embassy from the heavenly world visited the spot. Moses and Elijah, who figured so conspicuously in the solemn transactions on Sinai, were seen talking together. They had never before met on earth, but they had a mission to perform, in connection with the glorious enterprise of human redemption, which Christ on the three mountains determined successively to unfold and accomplish.

The Jewish law-giver had been dead about fifteen hundred years. The Lord had buried him in a valley over against Bethpeor; but no human eye was permitted to witness his mysterious dissolution, and no man knoweth of his sepulchre unto this day. He was the first penman employed to write the volume of inspiration, the deliverer of the Jews from bondage, the king in Jeshurun, the prophet, and the type of Christ. Here he appeared with the Saviour, in the Transfiguration, to testify to His Messiahship, and to do Him homage as the world's great prophet, and man's Redeemer. Elijah had been eminently honored in not tasting death, but had been translated to heaven, in a chariot of fire, about nine hundred years previously. He had descended to bear testimony to Christ, and of the world unseen. Both these servants of the Lord had been distinguished for extraordinary piety, zeal, and usefulness. They had alike fasted forty days, and were signal instruments in the hand of God. The one appeared as the representative of the Law, and the other as the representative of the Prophets. The types and the antitype were brought into juxtaposition,— the servants doing homage to the Master, in whom the Law and the Prophets were fulfilled. These two heavenly ambassadors were also representatives of the equal splendor of the quick and dead at the second advent. Moses represented the myriads who shall rise from their graves; and Elias, those who shall be found alive upon the earth, and changed in the twinkling of an eye.

But how did the disciples recognize these illustrious personages? Did they hear Jesus call them by their names? Then how must they have felt astonished at the information. They must have felt almost as if the earth had given way beneath them, and eternity had overtaken them unawares. Never, since the catastrophe of the Fall, had the glory of the invisible world been so exhibited. The association was the most dignified and sublime, that had ever fallen to the lot of mortals to witness. There was the Son of the eternal love, clothed in majesty; two celestial visitors from the city of God; the Apostles Peter, James, and John; and doubtless attendant angels, all enchanted with the scene of the Transfiguration.

The topic of discourse, in which the embassy were so absorbingly interested, was the death of Christ, which He should accomplish at Jerusalem. They called His death a *decease*, as if they would comfort Him with the expression, and present to His mind the glory that should follow. They probably spoke of its necessity, to realize types and fulfil prophecies; its merit and preciousness, in promoting our peace and restoration to the Divine favor; its influence, in spoiling the powers of Satan, and opening the kingdom of heaven to all believers; and the reward that Christ should receive in the eternal approbation of the Father, and in the honors and praises of the redeemed forever. They spoke of His decease as the most interesting subject to Christ, the most important to man, and the most glorious to God.

The grandeur of the Transfiguration had reached its height. The atmosphere was heavenly. The disciples were pleased, and profited with the proofs of their Master's divinity. St. Peter said to Jesus, in accents of love and tenderness, "Lord, it is good for us to be here. If thou wilt, let us make here three tabernacles; one for thee, and one for Moses, and one for Elias." It does not appear that he wished to build four, or six; only three. He probably expected to be received into the one with Jesus, or was willing, with his brethren, to stand at a distance. But the Holy Ghost declared that he knew not what he said. He knew that heaven was near, and that God was revealing Himself; and while he looked bewildered on the forms before him, his unconscious lips murmured forth the feelings of his heart. The request was the result of feeling, simply, and not of judgment. He forgot that they were only on a mountain-top. He lost sight of the multitude above, whom no man can number, and was unmindful of the solemn topic of discourse,—that Christ was to suffer death. Had his proposal been accepted, the eternal interests of our race would have been forever lost.

Up to this time, all had felt indescribably happy. But suddenly the manifestation assumed a new and singular phenomena. "A bright cloud overshadowed them." This was strikingly significant. Unlike the cloud that rested on Sinai at the giving of the Law, dark and portentous, the cloud on Tabor carried no rolling thunder; no lightnings flashed from it, but it was bright and glittering, as if the sun shone behind it, intimating the graciousness and clearness of the era, which had then commenced. It was the Shekinah, or divine habitation, affording evidence that Christ is present with His people, militant and triumphant, the theme of both, the song of both, the life of both. The family of Christ is one, and He is the soul of its existence, and the bond of its union.

From the bright foldings of that cloud there sounded a voice which said, " This is my beloved Son, in whom I am well pleased; hear ye Him." It was the voice of Him, who sitteth upon the throne, between the cherubim, and who clothes Himself with light as with a garment, — the voice of the everlasting Father clothed in human language, — the voice out of heaven, prophetic of that declaration, "The tabernacle of God is with men, and He will dwell with them; and they shall be His people; and God Himself shall be with them, and be their God." It was an attesting voice, attesting the dignity and divine mission of the Saviour as coequal with the Father, "Lord of all, and God over all, blessed forever." It was an approving voice, expressive of deep affection, with a richness and peculiarity of meaning, that can apply equally to no other being in heaven, or, on earth. It was an instructive voice: "Hear Him." We must hear Christ as He speaks in His word, as He speaks in His example, as He speaks in His Church. We must listen with simplicity and meekness, with faith and attention. "He that hath ears to hear, let him hear."

The mountain scene of Christ's glory became too grand for weakly human nature. The rapture of the disciples was exchanged for fear. "They fell on their faces, and were sore afraid. And Jesus came and touched them, and said,

Arise, and be not afraid." What gushing of fervent sympathy and melting tenderness accompanied this expression! What an infusion of vigor and buoyancy did they receive from His sacred touch! One touch of Christ is enough for restoration. "If I may but touch the hem of His garment," said one, "I shall be made whole." He is the Sun of Righteousness, with healing in His wings.

The Transfiguration at length ceased. The splendor that beamed forth was removed. Moses and Elias returned to the other world. The mountain became as it was before,— cold, solitary, and silent. The wind played among the rustling foliage. The stars rose one after another, and twinkled in the distant firmament. The silvery moon poured her light over the darkened landscape. And as the disciples lifted up their wondering eyes, "they saw no man save Jesus only."

The interesting incidents of the vision, while they served to unfold and establish the solemn sanctions on Sinai, were specially designed to be preparatory to the awful tragedy that was shortly to be enacted on Calvary. The Son of God was on His way to the Metropolis. The cross was already in His eye, and He was invigorated, by what had just transpired, to meet the approaching trial. The night-piece of His passion combined the tragical and horrible in an appalling degree. "He was despised and rejected of men." "The ploughers ploughed upon His back, and made long their furrows." "He gave His back to the smiters, and His cheeks to them that plucked off the hair: He hid not His face from shame and spitting." All this was minutely accomplished, when Pilate took Jesus and scourged Him, and the soldiers platted a crown of thorns, and put it on His head. The scourging and the thorn-crowning were a disgrace and infamy that might rend even nerves of steel. The punishment was the more severe, probably, because it was intended to be equivalent to crucifixion, though it afterwards proved to be only introductory to it. The ridicule and mockery heaped on Him were of the bitterest, and most poignant kind. Heaven would certainly have interfered, but for the compassion which it bore for the murderers. The sentence of condemnation, based upon false charges, was hastily pronounced, and every precaution adopted by His adversaries to carry it promptly into effect. But the suffering Saviour was not surprised by the raging storm. He knew that His hour was come, and was prepared to welcome it. The tide of love that floated Him into the world buoyed Him up for the crisis, and made it His meat to "do the will of Him that sent Him, and to finish His work."

Consigned to the ignominy of a public execution, it was arranged that He should die on Calvary, with two malefactors, who had violated the laws of their country, and were to suffer the retribution of civil justice. The three individuals are elevated on their several crosses, alike exposed to the general execration. But it is Jesus, who occupies the central position, that attracts so much attention. It is principally to witness His end, that so many persons have come together. All sorts and conditions of men are assembled to behold the sight. All are more or less anxious concerning Him; some in one way, some in another. Several conflicting opinions are openly expressed; but the great mass of the people, destitute of the ordinary feelings of humanity, mock His dying agonies. Shouts, taunts, and fierce blasphemies, ruffle that sea of faces now turned toward Him. But were our eyes unsealed, as were those of the prophet's servant, we should discern, beside and above that howling rabble, a more august gathering. Legions of spirits, whose feeblest warriors would have turned to paleness the cheek of Cæsar, are gazing with intense solicitude, but withheld from interposing by some dread prohibition. Angels that excel in strength are watching that desolate sufferer with adoring interest. Those invisible beings that smote Sennacherib's camp, and slew the first-born of Egypt, have often bowed before Him as their Creator and Lord. The sovereign Ruler of the universe yields this passive obedience to His moral subjects, for a sublime result. The King of glory endures the ignominy of the cross, that we might have everlasting life. "He was cut off, but not for Himself;" "died for our sins," "made His soul an offering for sin," "was made sin for us," "bare our sins in His body on the tree." "He was wounded for our transgressions, and bruised for our iniquities"; suffered the penalty incurred by our guilt, bore the punishment that we deserved as sinners, paid all that we owed as creatures, and made us the joyful inheritors of the results of His cross and passion. It is written, "Christ tasted death for every man." "He died for all." "He gave Himself a ransom for all." "He is the propitiation for our sins; and not for ours only, but for the sins of the whole world." Just as certainly as one is compelled to acknowledge that he is a sinner, so assuredly may he exult in the confidence that Christ came to save him. It is the will of God our Saviour, that all men should be saved, and come to the knowledge of the truth. He is not willing that any should perish, but that all should come to repentance.

The death of Christ is very beautifully described as an atonement. "We joy in God through our Lord Jesus Christ, by whom we have received the atonement." The origin of the word is to make two at one — at-one-ment; to bring two, that were separate from each other, into oneness of communion. Hence Christ is said to have reconciled Jew and Gentile unto God, in one body by the cross. "God hath reconciled us to Himself by Jesus Christ." "God was in Christ, reconciling the world to Himself." The yawning chasm between earth and heaven is bridged by His atoning merits. The shores of the severed land are reunited. The new and living way, which He has consecrated for us by His blood, lies over Calvary. The length of the road adds to the traveller's strength. The faster he walks, the stronger he feels. If he run, he is not weary. When he walks, he is not faint. "Wait on the Lord: be of good courage, and He shall strengthen thine heart."

There is afforded us on Calvary the noblest expression of God's love, in its tenderest and sweetest form. "Herein is love, not that we loved God, but that He loved us, and sent His

Son to be the propitiation of our sins." The death of Christ was not the cause, but the evidence, of God's love, and the only apparent channel, by which it could reach and reclaim us. The blessings of salvation come to us through Him. There is no other name given under heaven, whereby we can be saved. None have entered into rest, but through the merits of Christ. He is the last hope of all who have died in the Lord; the last object, on which departed saints fixed their gaze in this world, and the first, on which it fastened in the realms of glory.

The compassionate Jehovah has done everything, which mercy prompted, to melt down human obduracy, and win the affections. The heart must be harder than adamant, that does not soften and relent under such overwhelming demonstrations of kindness and love. The boon of salvation is placed within the reach of all who will come to the altar of propitiation, and plead the merits of Him, who bled and died. The path to the skies is cleared of obstructions. The doors of the kingdom of heaven are flung wide open: and death is swallowed up of victory. Oh, if there is one spot on this wide earth more sacred than another, it is Mount Calvary. Its moral altitude no mortal eye can measure; and its moral grandeur is connected with mysteries and revelations, that will cause a brightness to be reflected from its summit, when all other mountains shall melt in the general ruin. The continuous lesson, which it inculcates, is "Christ crucified." This is the true theology, the clew to the obscurest mysteries, the key-note to a thousand songs. Christ crucified, was the finisher of redemption. Of the people there were none with Him. "His own arm brought salvation." Christ crucified is the spiritual Founder, the sovereign Head, and preserver of His Church. She is the purchase of His blood, the reflection of His glory, the object of His love. "He shall build the temple of the Lord; He shall bear the glory." Christ crucified is the theme of the holy ministry. "We preach not ourselves, but Christ Jesus the Lord." "Whom we preach, warning every man, and teaching every man in all wisdom, that we may present every man perfect in Christ Jesus." Christ crucified is the light and blessedness of heaven. Angels, and principalities, and powers hang on the slain Lamb for their existence and happiness. Christ crucified is the burden of the song of the redeemed. "Worthy is the Lamb that was slain to receive power and riches, and wisdom, and strength, and honor, and glory, and blessing."

In the light of heaven we shall see the glorified Redeemer as He is. Not as He was, the object of human scorn, the victim of cruel malignity. Not as He was, when climbing the heights of Tabor, or descending its slopes. Not as He was in the garden of Gethsemane, overwhelmed with an agony, that baptized Him in His own blood. Not as He was, in the hands of the Jewish authorities, bound with cords, mocked, buffeted, spat upon, crowned with thorns. Not as He was, bearing His cross to Calvary, crucified, taunted with scornful breath, pierced with the soldier's spear, and laid in Joseph's tomb. No. We shall see Him as He is, having "on His head many crowns, and on

His vesture, and on His thigh a name written, King of kings, and Lord of lords." We shall see Him as He is, in all the splendor and majesty of the Godhead, in all the glory, and grandeur, and enjoyment of heaven. We shall see Him as He is, receiving the greetings and hosannas of the glorified, all singing from the overflowings of their gratitude, " Unto Him that loved us, and washed us from our sins in His own blood, and hath made us kings and priests unto God, and the Father, to Him be glory and dominion for ever and ever. Amen."

## THE THREE LOVED ONES OF BETHANY.

"Now Jesus loved Martha, and her sister, and Lazarus." They were eminently pious and devout individuals. They had often ministered to Him of their substance; and He had as frequently repaid them by the higher consolations, which He so generously distributed. The manifold actions of His life were just so many instances of goodness and benevolence, resembling the full ripe fruits of Autumn, amid the numerous leaves and petals that surround them. Wherever He went He displayed the most winning smiles and condescending love. When He stretched out His hands, it was to scatter blessings. When He opened His lips, it was to dispense words of instruction and comfort. When He made excursions through the country, they were missions of mercy. Though sinless, He was a man of sorrows and acquainted with grief, and found those among the circle of His followers, with whom He enjoyed that near attachment, and familiar interchange of thought and feeling, peculiar to the intimacies and fellowship of kindred minds. After the toils and travels of the day, in the vicinity of Jerusalem, He would often pause and refresh Himself at Bethany, and find a congenial atmosphere, and a welcome retreat. With the members of this pious family He would commune in the unchecked gushings of His heart, and reciprocate the cordialities of their friendship, pure and changeless. While they washed His weary feet, He would discourse to them of His works of mercy, and the kingdom of blessedness and peace, which He was about to establish. They listened to His sacred voice with breathless attention, and counted it their highest happiness to be deemed worthy the notice of a Being so illustrious. It was well perhaps that they had not a more overwhelming disclosure of His ineffable majesty: for had they been fully aware of the flood of light and glory, that lay concealed under the garb of humanity, they might have feared to receive Him. They had seen fully enough to assure them that His credentials were heavenly, and were bold to entertain Him as their guest, when the heads of the nation were conspiring to kill Him. Never was their cottage so dignified, as when thus hallowed by His personal presence. Never had they a friend so dear, as when the Wonderful, the Counsellor, the Prince of Peace, bestowed on them the fulness of His love, and opened up to them the depths of His heart.

The domestic scenes of the household illustrate very beautifully the variations and shades of character, which that family exhibited. The two sisters, and their brother appeared to constitute the whole of the circle. They had their peculiar dispositions and imperfections; yet they were a Christian family, and "fellow-heirs of the grace of life."

Martha was active and impulsive, naturally ardent, and a little petulant; susceptible of domestic vanity and ostentation. She may not have been worldly, or covetous; only over-careful about much serving, and anxious, as the mistress of the house, to make an unnecessary and expensive entertainment. There would seem to be a want of prudence and politeness in some of her actions. She broke in upon our Lord's discourse, and requested Him to send Mary to her assistance. But the Saviour, knowing the kindness of her heart, replied with a mildness and majesty of reproof, " Martha, Martha, thou art careful and troubled about many things; but one thing is needful, and Mary hath chosen that good part which shall not be taken away from her."

Mary was of a contemplative turn of mind, full of pleasing emotion, and disposed to embrace every opportunity for religious improvement. Thoughtful and inquiring, she was happy to sit at the Saviour's feet, and listen to the gracious words that dropped from His lips. She was of a calmer temperament than Martha, and was the subject of an elevated devotional piety. Her virtues were transparent; and while all could see in them the pure blue sky of heaven's sunshine, they failed not to diffuse a halo of glory over the place, that was the scene of her residence. There is something beautiful in the allusion to Bethany, as the town of Mary and her sister Martha. It may possibly have derived celebrity from other events; from the exploits of heroes, poets, and philosophers; and that if you had asked some native Rabbi what constituted its greatest fame, he would point to yon tall, tapering spire, to some exquisite specimen of architectural grandeur, or deeds of patriotism enshrined in the hearts of the people. But these are adventitious distinctions, of little account in the estimation of Heaven. The sounds of human applause cease to be heard before they reach the skies; while the sigh of a broken heart, and the petition of a contrite spirit ascend to God swifter than an angel's wing, and higher than an angel's pinion can possibly soar. The great things of earth are pressed by the light of heaven into a small space; and the little things of the world are mighty, because they are moral, and associated with the glory of God, and the good of souls. The circumstance so remarkable in the history of Bethany, which gave it consideration at the time, and that will cause its memorial to continue till the latest generation, was that Martha, Mary, and Lazarus were natives of it. These three fair and fragrant flowers were, in the sight of God, the most beautiful things it contained. These three devoted saints gave an attraction to the place, causing the fame of heroes, and the hymns of poets to be unnoticed, and unsung. We should suppose if anywhere, the aching head could rest, and the weary heart could beat in stillness, — if anywhere, home-born joys would nestle and flutter, and sickness should not prey, and death itself should be an exile,—it would be that home in Bethany, which Jesus so signally honored, and whose inmates and tenants were His faithful and devoted friends. But "all things come alike to all; there is one event to the righteous, and to the wicked, to the good, and to the clean, and the unclean; to him that sacrificeth, and to him that sacrificeth not." Sickness enters alike the house of the Christian and the worldling. The stroke of bereavement befalls the one, equally with the other. Lazarus, an old disciple, much attached to Christ, and much beloved by Him, was suddenly smitten by disease, while Christ was far away preaching to the multitude of Bethabara, beyond Jordan. "Therefore the sisters sent unto Him saying, Lord, behold he whom thou lovest is sick." They presumed, probably, that if they made His affection for him the basis of their appeal, it would insure a prompt and speedy compliance with their wishes. The wondrous theme of Christ's love is at any time the most successful plea that can be urged. His love is not like ours, frail and evanescent, fickle and inconstant, but deep and abiding, disinterested and permanent, — like the hill-side springs, unaffected by winter's cold, or summer's heat.

Though the Saviour knew of this sickness, before the arrival of the messenger to announce it, yet He did not immediately hasten thither, but "tarried two days still in the same place where He was." This is one of His methods of answering prayer. He takes his own time, and sends the blessing when it will accomplish the most benefit to the petitioner, and the greatest glory to Himself. "This sickness," said He, is not unto death, but for the glory of God, that the Son of God might be glorified thereby." He understood perfectly, at a distance, the disease, with its symptoms and results. He knows the malady under which *we* are laboring, and the sin which most easily besets us. His omniscient eye penetrates all vails, searches out every prejudice, disentangles every passion, and detects at the very root the defalcation and the blight, that wither and lay us low.

The Holy Jesus turned His face toward Bethany, accompanied by His inquiring disciples, who marvelled at His strange language concerning the departed Lazarus. "Our friend Lazarus sleepeth; but I go that I may awake him out of sleep." The dust of the sleeping saint belongs to Jesus; and it is His prerogative to remodel and raise it up again, instinct with life. The believer in Christ dies not like other men, but sweetly falls asleep until the resurrection morn. It is the sleep, not of unconsciousness, but of refreshment and rest; the sleep of the laborer after the fatigues of the day; the sleep of the soldier after the combats of the battle; the sleep of the traveller after the toils of his journey; the sleep of repose in Jesus, consecrated and blessed. " And if we believe that Jesus died and rose again, even so them also which sleep in Jesus, will God bring with Him." " I shall be satisfied," said David, " when I awake, with thy likeness."

The afflicted Martha, when she heard that Christ had come within the precincts of the town, went forth to meet Him, and looking into His placid face, exclaimed, with emotions of sorrow and affection, " Lord, if thou hadst been here, my brother had not died. Thy brother shall rise again," He replied. Though doubtful of the exact import of this calm assurance, yet confiding in His Almighty power, she hastened to call Mary, who sat disconsolate in the house. The intelligence, " The Master is come, and calleth for thee," fell like music on her ears, and she ran quickly to embrace Him. The title Master belongs supremely to Christ. And O what a master for kindness, love, and sympathy! Jesus wept at the scene of lamentation; yea, "groaned in spirit, and was troubled." What agitation seemed for a moment to convulse that sacred bosom! What tossing of emotion! What mastery of love! Bending over the grave of the lost one, He cried with a voice so loud, "Lazarus come forth," that the dead instantly obeyed, the blood began to liquefy, the pulse began to beat, the motionless heart grew warm, the color mantled the cheek, the living soul was recalled, and the buried friend came forth, bound hand and foot with grave-clothes, and his face bound about with a napkin. They loosed him from his grave habiliments to live again, and die. How long this second lease of earthly existence was continued, we know not, nor how frequent the interviews which he enjoyed with the Resurrection and the Life. We are only informed that he was restored to the society of the living, and that he once more filled up the gap in that little group, which death had so unfeelingly torn open.

There happened, a few days before the last Passover, another occasion, when Jesus went to Bethany in company with some of His disciples.

He arrived in the village just as the sabbath was closing. The day had been one of rest, and leisure, and devout rejoicing. The Saviour was expected. A supper was prepared for Him. He was to be the guest of Lazarus and his sisters; and friends and neighbors were invited to meet Him. The meal was to be taken in the house of Simon the leper, perhaps, because it was more commodious, allowing them to share equally the honor of receiving so dignified a personage. Simon was not a leper at that time, or he would have been under legal restraint, and none would have been allowed to hold intercourse with him. But he had been a leper, and was cured, probably, by the interposition of the Saviour, and therefore as a token of regard and gratitude, he was desirous of entertaining his benefactor. As the evening proceeded, the company was startled by a remarkable incident, that arrested their attention. Mary, looking at the Master as He lay on the couch, rose up and went behind Him, and taking an alabaster box of ointment of spikenard very precious, about a pound weight, broke the seal that secured it, and poured it on His head. The company was taken by surprise, and the house was filled with the odor of the ointment. It was an act of love, and gratitude, and respect, that had doubtless long been premeditated. She had kept it by her for some time, and now that the fitting opportunity was afforded, the hoarded treasure, and the hoarded love were poured out at the same time. The sacrifice was considerable, and would have been difficult to accomplish, but for the overflowing fulness of her heart. She may possibly have purchased this costly perfume to expend upon the charms of her person. But the fervor of her attachment to the Lord, reduced the value of other attraction, and caused her to forget all thoughts of herself in the thoughts of her Saviour.

The use of unction in Judea was a delicious indulgence, and when bestowed on another was always considered a token of honor. " Ointment and perfume rejoice the heart." "Let thy head lack no ointment," said Solomon. And David, when speaking of the munificence of the Divine goodness, says, "Thou anointest my head with oil, and my cup runneth over." The excellency of brotherly love is compared to the precious ointment poured upon the head of Aaron, that ran down his beard, and flowed to the lowest borders and fringes of his garments. The force of these allusions is not so obviously felt in this country as in the climates of the East. Yet there are few who would like to be thought insensible to the charms of fragrance, and the adaptations of the productions of Nature to regale and delight the senses. We are generously supplied with softness and smoothness for the touch, with colors for the eye, with melodies for the ear, with relishes for the taste, and with odors for the smell. There is profusion without extravagance, and richness without satiety.

There were some present, who witnessed the service of Mary, that felt indignation. They murmured at what they considered a waste, as if it were possible that anything could be wasted on the person of Christ. Some calculated the value of the ointment, and fixed its worth at three hundred pence, or forty-five dollars. Judas asked why it could not have been sold for this sum, "and given to the poor: not that he cared for the poor, but because he was a thief, and had the bag." The Saviour, commenting upon the circumstance, pronounced it a good work. "Wheresoever this gospel shall be preached," said He, "throughout the world, this also that she hath done, shall be told for a memorial of her." The prediction is fulfilled. It is recorded in Holy Writ. It is preached in church. It receives an absolute and universal dissemination. There was more embodied in that personal act, than the parties present were disposed to acknowledge. It was an intimation and prefiguration of the Saviour's death. The anointing was for His burial. He was then ready to be offered, and the time of His suffering was at hand. This was His last visit to Bethany before His crucifixion. Though it is not certain, or probable that Mary intended emblematically to solemnize the event, yet it afforded an instance of the overruling Providence of God, who in the performance of an enterprise, has frequently an end in view, far beyond the knowledge and design of the agent.

The prominent feature of admiration in the history of the family of Bethany, was their cordial reciprocation of Divine love. Jesus loved Martha, Mary, and Lazarus; and the affection He bore for them flowed lovingly back to its source and centred in its origin. Christ's love is the life-blood that circulates through all the veins and arteries of His redeemed and chosen people. It creates the glow of summer in the soul, and is no less clear, and calm, and strong, than it is genial and warm. The heart can be subject to no influence richer in the purest enjoyment. If the heart be contracted, this will enlarge it; if it be dormant, it will excite it to action; if it be glowing, it will kindle its fervor. Its tendency is to mould insensibly the character to the image of the object loved, that, " beholding as in a glass the glory of the Lord," we may be " changed into the same image, from glory to glory, by the Spirit of the Lord." The conformity, as far as it prevails, makes us one with Christ, identifying our interest with His interest, and service, and glory. Nor ought it to be forgotten that the love of Christ's admirers grows more intense the more they suffer and do for Him. Every little service undertaken, and performed on His account, every contribution to His treasury, and every effort for His glory, has the effect of strengthening our attachment to the Lord, and His cause. It takes away from the world to come the awful strangeness of a new sphere, and a new state of existence, and sheds over it a home feeling. When we come to its margin, we are not lonely and solitary, but cheered by kindred and friends. The Saviour's love reciprocated, forms our introduction to glory, and finds in heaven its element and its home.

The removal of Lazarus by death, impressively assures us that the holiest and most devoted families are liable to changes, losses, and bereavements. The fair sky of the sunniest circles may be shrouded in the blackness of night. The air-castles, which were thought to be secure, are suddenly dissipated; and the dearest and best of friends swept into the dust of the grave. Whom the Lord loves best, He sometimes takes the soonest. The son of Jeroboam, who alone of that family had something good in him toward the Lord God of Israel, was called to an early tomb. Even where the removal of God's servants has not been so premature, the transition has been so instantaneous as to surprise them into blessedness. The king of terrors comes, not as an enemy, but as a friend; not as a penalty, but as a blessing. The Apostle places death in the same category as the enjoyment of life. "All things are yours, whether life or *death.*" The reason for so merciful a change in its character, is that Christ has " abolished death, and brought life and immortality to light." He has passed through the terrible ordeal before us, grappling with all its horrors, extracting all its bitterness, and now gives it back to us clad in a robe of radiant lustre, holding a broken sceptre in one hand, and a wreath in the other, with which to crown us with victory and triumph.

We are indebted to Bethany for the Saviour's definition of true godliness. " One thing is needful." True religion is one, — one in its author, one in its end, one in the aggregate,— but made up of many ingredients. Whether it be wisdom, the fear of the Lord, a new heart, a new creature, or the incorruptible seed, these are only so many names of one and the same thing. The human body consists of many members, but it is one body. The Mississippi is fed by many tributaries, but it is one river. Yon beautiful tree has many roots below, and branches above, but it is one vegetable form. The religion of the cross is comprehensive in its requirements, but is one beautiful and harmonious whole. "One thing have I desired of the Lord," said the Psalmist, "that will I seek after, that I may dwell in the house of the Lord all the days of my life, to behold the beauty of the Lord, and to inquire in His temple." And said St. Paul, "This one thing I do, forgetting the things that are behind, and reaching forth to those that are before, I press toward the mark for the prize of the high calling of God, in Christ Jesus." The cheerful pursuit of this one thing, is the brightest feature in our sad and sinful lot. There is nothing else that will repay our assiduity. All other objects that we toil for, are mere spangles and tinsels, dust and dross, bubbles colored with rainbow hues, that collapse at a touch, and when they burst, smart the eyes of the child that blows them. We have tried the experiments of the world; and if we try them again, we shall be but the victims of an aching disappointment and vanity. 'T will be the same as chasing a gaudy insect, and when it is clasped, we shall find its brightest hues to be brushed away, and it will perish in our hand. 'T will be to nurse a flower, upon which the blight and the mildew will fall, and it will wither in our presence. 'T will be to repose beneath a tree, on which the lightning and the thunderbolt will descend, and it will be blasted on the heath. It will be to cherish in our bosoms a viper, which we can only warm and vivify, that it may sting us to the heart.

The ideal of bliss which the wand of fancy may prefigure, will never be realized till we cease to expect it from the lying vanities of the world. But when we give up the search, sit at the feet of Jesus, and love and serve Him, we have joy and peace in believing. The objects of earthly ambition, which we once thought so desirable, now dwindle into nothingness, and seem to us as far below the blessings of salvation as the loftiest Alps appear beneath the sun. The one thing needful is supreme. It enters into the very essence of our happiness, takes in the whole circuit of our interest, respects the body and the soul, and has "the promise of the life that now is, and of that which is to come." Other things are only subordinately needful; this is preëminently so. Other things are only occasionally needful; this is invariably so. Other things are only needful for certain individuals; this is needful for all.

> "More needful this than glittering wealth,
> Or aught the world bestows;
> Not reputation, food, or health,
> Can give us such repose."

## THE THREE CHOSEN DISCIPLES.

> " Strong in the great Redeemer's name,
> They bore the Cross, despised the shame;
> And, like their Master here,
> Wrestled with danger, pain, distress;
> Hunger, and cold, and nakedness,
> And every form of fear;
> To feel His love their only joy;
> To tell that love their sole employ."

THE purest affection is susceptible of degrees of fervor toward the objects of its regard. Christ had His intimate companions, and bosom friends. The chosen witnesses of some of His most sacred scenes were Peter, James, and John. They were His only attendants when He raised the daughter of Jairus to life; the favored three that were permitted to be with Him on the Mount of Transfiguration; and the special observers of His agony in the Garden of Gethsemane. There never was a group probably more united by the ties of affection, or more dissimilar in their natural temperament.

If the historical record be correct, Simon Peter was a man of strong and muscular energy; his eye dark, his complexion full and sallow, his character harsh and abrupt, and his general movements particularly impulsive. Of his early history nothing very remarkable has been handed down to us. He was the son of Jonas, born at Bethsaida, a small fishing-town on the western shore of the Lake of Tiberius. His original name was Simon, which his Divine Master changed for Cephas, when He called him to the Apostleship. Cephas is a Syriac name, signifying a stone or rock. It reads in Latin *petra*, from which is derived Peter, meaning the same thing. As a derivative, it suggests only a fragment, or part of a rock—simply a stone. St. Peter was to be one of the Apostles, upon whose ministry the Church of the New Testament was to be founded. She is " built on the foundation of the apostles and prophets, Jesus Christ himself being the chief corner-stone."

After his marriage Peter lived with his wife,

and mother-in-law, in a house at Capernaum, a short distance from his birthplace, on the shore of the same lake. His brother Andrew was a disciple of John the Baptist, and called to a knowledge of the Saviour prior to himself. Andrew was present when the venerable forerunner pointed his audience to Jesus, and said, " Behold the Lamb of God, that taketh away the sin of the world." No sooner was he permitted to see and converse with the incarnate Saviour, than he felt naturally anxious to dispense to those he loved, something of the gratitude and joy, with which his own heart was overflowing with the discovery. " And first finding his own brother Simon, he saith unto him, We have found the Messias : and he brought him to Jesus." This was the commencement of Peter's biography. It took its date from the hour when, by the active exertions of a brother's love, he was brought to the Saviour's feet.

The two brothers passed one day in company with the Lord Jesus, and then, taking their leave of Him for a season, returned to their ordinary occupation of fishing. It does not appear that Simon Peter became one of the Saviour's constant attendants at that time, or that he felt himself immediately called upon to devote himself, heart and soul, to the labors of the Apostleship. For a short period, at least, he continued to employ himself in his accustomed avocation, requiring a more distinct and explicit call, before entering upon the arduous duties and destinies that awaited him. It was probably about the end of that same year, when Andrew and himself had been fishing all night on the Sea without success, and were in the act of washing their nets, that Jesus entered into their ship, and desired them to launch out into the deep, and to let down their nets for a draught. The request was no sooner complied with, than the multitude of fishes taken was so immense that the nets brake, and their little bark began to sink, with the weight of them. The effect of this miracle was an overpowering impression of their unworthiness, which filled them with trepidation and alarm, when Jesus drew near to console them, and said unto Peter, "Fear not; henceforth thou shalt catch men." The trade to which he had devoted himself was to be instructive of holier lessons, and sublimer employments; and the unusually large draught of fishes just taken, was doubtless intended as an intimation of the yet greater success, which should attend his enterprise in fishing for souls when he should cast the Gospel net into the wide ocean. From that moment the Apostle could say, "Lo, we have left all and followed Thee"; "Lord to whom shall we go but unto Thee; Thou hast the words of eternal life." He was ardently attached to Christ, and being naturally impulsive, was sometimes rash in the expression of his love. Whatever feeling chanced to predominate, drew his whole soul along with it in one explosive act. The thoughts and feelings of his heart he openly expressed. His faith may not have been more wavering than that of his brethren, but it was intermittent. His intentions were good, but he was changeable.

There are few persons but have known in the course of their lives, one, or more individuals, equally fervent in protestation, and frail in action. The basis of their movements is generally a warm and overflowing earnestness, which makes them as ready and ample in their promises, as they are full and vehement in their emotions. But any one, whose only guide is a strong impulse, may be led into evil as well as good, with an ease and rapidity that astonish men of more tempered and tranquil minds. Energy of itself has no controlling power. We can no more look to it for guidance, than we can expect the tempest to bear a richly freighted ship, in a steady, onward direction. Persons of strong feelings are thus peculiarly exposed to the force of outward circumstances. They are borne hither, and thither by the breeze, which for the moment prevails. If there be no difficulties in the way, they run well. If temptations assail them, they speedily fall. And when a wrong step has once been taken, retreat is next to impossible. Such individuals generally sink as low, as they would have risen, under other circumstances.

The fall of Peter was in exact accordance

with his natural disposition. He had just protested, "I will lay down my life for Thy sake." "I am ready to go with Thee both to prison, and to death;" when Christ calmly replied, "Verily, I say unto thee, the cock shall not crow before thou shalt thrice deny that thou knowest me." The dreaded cloud had loomed up, and was ready to burst. Jesus was about to be apprehended, and led away to trial, and everything betokened a speedy destruction. The mind of this ardent disciple was buoyed up, amid all these dark signs, with the idea that his Lord would yet shine forth, in the splendor of His omnipotence, and smite his enemies with confusion. But when Jesus stood before the Sanhedrim, and all the power of the nation was arrayed against Him, the last hope of Peter took its flight, and he began to be in doubt. He followed his Master, with tottering steps, over the threshold of the open gate, that led to the courtyard, and set his feet on the scene of judgment. The damsel who kept the door, holding up the lantern to his face, regarded him with a look of suspicion, as though she knew him. To escape recognition, he turned partially aside, and hurried on as quickly as possible. The soldiers had kindled a fire, and were crowding around it; and Peter, with a careless mien, as if only anxious to warm himself, took his place among them. This was the act by which he committed himself; and it was perfectly inexcusable. The Lord had solemnly warned him that he would be guilty of denying Him that night. And it was not wise,—it was not justifiable, that he should thus cast himself into the furnace of temptation. Our safety consists in neither compromising, nor temporizing. We should resolve not to be found in such society. We should be able to say with David, "I will not know a wicked person;" and with Jacob, "O my soul, come not thou into their secret; unto their assembly, mine honor be not thou united." It was while seated among the servants in the hall that a damsel accused him of associating with the prisoner; and he denied before them all saying, "I know not what thou sayest." Scarcely had he time to congratulate himself on the success of his evasion, before another maid saw him, and said unto them that were there, "This fellow was also with Jesus of Nazareth. Then he denied with an oath, I do not know the man. After a while came unto him they that stood by, and said to Peter, Surely thou art also one of this man's disciples; for thy speech bewrayeth thee." Now all the energy of his soul was roused to repeat the denial, cursing and swearing, "I know not the man." One falsehood necessitated another, and led to oaths and curses. But the more violently he protested, the more certain were the mercenaries that they were not mistaken. The Roman clarion, with its echoes, greeted the morn. The cocks were crowing aloft through the yet sleeping city. Their shrill tones were heard in the palace. And no malefactor condemned to suffer execution, for the violated laws of his country, ever heard the prison bell strike the last hour of his existence, with half the agony of feeling with which that terrible cock-crowing rang through the ears of the fallen disciple. It pierced like a dart the soul of that guilty man, who staggered about, restless and fugitive, like a stricken and chased deer.

There is an alarmist of some kind or other addressed to us all. The broad field of Revelation presents appeals to every passion of our nature, — hope and fear, joy and sorrow, honor and disgrace. The Spirit and the Bride lift up their voice, in tones of authority and admonition, to repent, and do our first works, and cleave to the Lord. Providence echoes a warning note, in the sickness that wastes our frame, the sorrow that gnaws our heart, the withered joy, and the blighted hope; all tell us that we are creatures of a day, quivering like aspen leaves on the tree of mortality. Did we hear these voices aright, and harden not our hearts, we should recognize the voice of the Lord, and weep bitterly.

"The Lord turned, and looked upon Peter." This was enough. There were volumes in that look, that needed no interpreter. The Saviour uttered not a word, breathed not a syllable, lifted not a finger, but turned and looked. It was a piercing, penetrating look, that sent home the arrow of conviction and repentance, with assured success. It was a look of painful remembrance, reviving faded recollections, and calling instantly to his mind the word of the Lord, which said, " Before the cock crow thou shalt deny me thrice." It was a look of inexpressible power and gentle condemnation, acting as a sword to wound, and a balm to heal. It was a look of full and free forgiveness, and brought back to the fold of the good Shepherd the erring sheep. The moment that eye of tenderness and love met the fallen disciple's, it melted his heart to contrition, and forthwith gushed a flood of tears, which a quick and hasty step could hardly conceal from the mocking gaze of surrounding foes. The Lord's dying and loving look melts stony hearts, —

> The Saviour hanging on the tree,
>   In agonies and blood,
> Methought once turned His eyes on me,
>   As near His cross I stood.
>
> Sure never till my latest breath
>   Can I forget that look;
> It seemed to charge me with His death,
>   Though not a word He spoke.

> A second look He gave, which said,
> I freely all forgive;
> This blood is for thy ransom paid;
> I die that thou may'st live.

Meet the pitying eye of Jesus with confidence and love. The upward glance of your eye may be imploring; but the downward beaming of His eye will be forgiving. Other eyes may be closed, or withdrawn; the eye of the Lord rests on you ever, with ineffable delight and unslumbering affection.

We hear no more of Peter till the morning of the resurrection. The interval was a period of bitter grief. It is said that a tear glistened in his eye as long as he lived. The remembrance of his fall never left him, and his sincere contrition reinstated him in the confidence of his friends. He was tardy in visiting "the place where the Lord lay," because his previous treachery hung like weights on his feet. But when he reached the tomb, his indomitable energy naturally returned, and took him at once *into* the sepulchre, while the timid and affectionate John had only sufficient courage to stoop down, and look in from the outside.

The period soon arrived for our Blessed Lord to ascend to His Father, and He addressed to St. Peter the charge, " Feed my sheep." Obedient to the commission, he preached, in the Jewish Metropolis, Jesus and the resurrection. Everywhere, and to all, he spake with a firmness that nothing could subdue, and with a boldness that none could awe. The fruits of his labors were abundant. Three thousand of his audience, at the Pentecost, cried, " Men and brethren, what shall we do ? " His fame spread far and wide : and if his shadow fell on the sick, as he passed along the streets of Jerusalem, they were immediately healed.

To St. Peter was awarded the honor of opening the door of the church for the admission of the Gentiles ; and nobly did he carry into execution the work assigned him. But the crown of martyrdom was his recompense. He was crucified at Rome, with his head downwards, about thirty-three years after the death of his Lord and Master. One can hardly contemplate the stormy evening that closed the earthly career of this eminent Apostle, without offering the petition, From the bitter pains of martyrdom, good Lord deliver us. We would like, if it be the will of our heavenly Father, that the angel of death should visit us in his *gentlest* mood; and that when we hear the rustling of his wings at our side, we may be equipped for the flight, and chant as we ascend, and melt as we chant, into heaven's own light.

The two brothers, James and John, were brought up in the same little town of Bethsaida that gave birth to St. Peter. The place of their nativity formed the scene of many of our Saviour's miracles, where He so generously diffused the blessings of His hands. It was on behalf of these sons of Zebedee, that their mother went to Christ, worshipping Him, and desiring a certain thing of Him. "And He said unto her, What wilt thou? She saith unto Him, Grant that these my two sons may sit, the one on thy right hand, and the other on the left in thy kingdom." Of the subsequent history of St. James, much indeed is not said. He was present at the Ascension, and was the first of the twelve Apostles who suffered martyrdom for the testimony of Jesus. This was the James that was killed by the sword. The ambitious popularity of Herod Agrippa caused him to be seized and executed in the city of Jerusalem. The all-atoning Saviour, whom he confessed before the Jewish rabble, sustained him in the conflict, and received his disembodied spirit into the mansions of rest.

The beloved John was permitted to live to a more extended age. In the year A. D. 97, he was banished to the Isle of Patmos; though his exile from an earthly home, served only to lift him nearer to a heavenly one. An inner radiance was poured into his spirit that more than compensated for his external night. God made his afflictions beautiful, by weaving through them the rainbow of His mercy and love. The Church was sitting in sackcloth and ashes; and the courts of the sanctuary were wet with the tears, and red with the blood, of the holiest of her sons: but the Lord who reigned supreme, cleared the darkened sky, and opened up to His servant John the visions of her future triumph, which made the barren

Patmos a scene of richer manifestations than the glories of Tabor. Thus the darkest cloud was fringed with celestial lustre; and the calamity which threatened to be most crushing, unbosomed by degrees its latent mercies. After the death of Domitian, the Apostle returned from exile, and visited the churches. Jerome says, that when he was weakened by age, and unable to walk, his disciples carried him; and as his voice faltered, his constantly repeated injunction was, "My dear children, love one another."

St. John was a personification of love. He was a sample of that benignant piety which propitiates affection, and unites the brotherhood. It is scarcely possible to peruse his writings, without feeling ourselves in contact with amenity and benevolence, beyond the usual attainments of flesh and blood. Good-will to man, and love to the Master, are seen welling out in every page. The placidity and gentleness of his communications look as if his heart had never cooled since it lay on the Saviour's bosom. Like as when we look into the unruffled bay, and discern through its sleeping waters the tender seaweed that scarcely waves in the breezeless tide, we say, It is long since a storm was here : for if there had been a recent tempest, though the surface might by this time be smooth, yet the brine would be muddy, and the sea-plants would be tangled and torn ; so when we look into St. John's pellucid pages, we behold such meekness and love shining through them that we irresistibly feel, Blessed man! it is long since the last gust of passion ruffled thy tranquil breast. Whatever agitations once convulsed it, they have been lulled to sleep. The beloved disciple's privilege was to live near the Saviour; and the nearer he got to Him, the more beautifully he reflected His likeness; till at length he became so identified with his ascended Lord, that we are reminded not so much of John, as of Christ Himself.

We can recall occasions in our history, when we have sat at the open lattice, on a balmy summer's day, and the wandering breeze wafted in a freight of some pleasant odor; and as it spread richly around, and drowned us with delight, we wondered what it was, and whence it came, till we recognized the scent of some favorite flower, that blossomed not far away. And there have been moments of surprisals, when we have been equally beguiled with the society of persons, in whom the Spirit of the Redeemer breathes. Our souls have been happy, and we have scarcely known why, till we remembered the open lattice, and the Rose of Sharon hard by; and as the south wind was fleeting past, why should not the spices flow? Such unequivocal outgoings of loveliness and affection from renewed souls, afford the noblest spectacle, upon which to rest our admiration, in this false and deceitful world. It is the religion of grace that makes one gracious; and the raiment of needlework, in its graceful arrangements, and colors, and perfume, which suggest to us the ivory palaces, and the fields, which the Lord hath blessed. But in order to be loved, we must be lovable. We must have not only grace in the heart, but grace in the lips, and the beauty of holiness in the life.

There was a notion current among the Jews that St. John was never to die. It arose from a misunderstanding of our Lord's words, — "If I will that he tarry till I come, what is that to thee? Yet Jesus said not unto him, he shall not die, but if I will that he tarry till I come, what is that to thee?" There is reason to believe that he died in the city of Ephesus, about the beginning of the second century. The last thirty years of his life were the most eventful in the Church's history. It was during this period that all the Apostles, except himself, were removed from the world, and their flocks committed to their successors. His own little circle of sympathy and attachment had been broken up. St. Peter was crucified at Rome; James was slain with the sword, at Jerusalem; and John was ready to breathe his last in the city of Ephesus.

The three disciples were so many bright specimens of Christianity, of whom the world was not worthy. They were natives of the same town, brought up to the same calling, and possessed excellencies in common, which attached them to the Lord, and to each other. Neither of them was wanting in any of the fruits of the Spirit, though each exhibited some feature of the Christian character more prominently than the others. If Peter was impulsive and energetic, James was calm and collected, and John was affectionate.

This little band of brothers is presented to our view for imitation. They were eminently Christ-loving disciples,— with Christ, for Christ, on the side of Christ, and fighting for His cause. " Be ye followers of them who through faith and patience inherit the promises." Try and catch their mantle. Fear not to adhere to Jesus too closely; nor to rejoice in Him too much. Let the love of God your Saviour flow in a full tide upon your cold and wintry souls; and it will cause them to burst into blossom, and fruit, and beauty. Christ's love is the balm of life. His presence the antidote of death. His glory the joy of heaven.

## THE THREE TEMPTATIONS.

THE infinite Jehovah appears, in the person of Christ, in softened splendor. He is as the sun shining behind a thin cloud, which, while it neither conceals nor obscures, enables us to contemplate Him with calmness and spiritual profit. It is no less as man, than as God, that Jesus is suited to our fallen race. If it were necessary that He should be Almighty, in order to redeem; it was also important that He should be all-merciful in order to sympathize. "Made," therefore, "in all things like unto His brethren, that He might be a faithful and merciful High-Priest, He was tempted in all points like as we are, yet without sin." The various species of assault that bore so heavily upon Him, from beneath and around, left Him untainted, and untouched in every particular. The world, the flesh and the devil, could find nothing in Him that was combustible; because He was that Holy thing, begotten of the Spirit of God. Neither the thought, nor the propensity of evil could find an entrance into His spotless mind. He felt no lusting of the flesh against the spirit, nor the slightest injection of unhallowed desire. All that the enemy could do against a heart so pure, was to propose external temptation to the senses, to ensnare and beguile. Accordingly, we read of one of the most daring attacks upon unoffending innocence, unsurpassed in the annals of history; one of the most wonderful and beneficial combats ever known, and one of the most glorious conquests ever achieved.

The Saviour had just received the Holy Rite of Baptism on the banks of the Jordan. He had just fulfilled all righteousness, and secured for that sacred Institution the approbation of the Trinity. He had now made a preparation for the commencement of the public duties of His ministry; and, being full of the Holy Ghost, retired into the wilderness, to mature, by prayer and fasting, the arrangements for the establishment of His kingdom, which should prove the ruin of His adversary. In that rugged and lonely desert, the Son of God endured a wonderful and supernatural fast, in which, for forty days, He ate nothing. Fasting was a part of the plan of redemption, to which He had devoted His life. It was a mean to an end, which He assiduously improved, in anticipation of the solemn scenes that were about to follow. Released from the toils of Nazareth, the Holy Jesus found a sacred occupation amid dry ravines, and staring precipices; the haunt of the satyr, and the nest of the vulture. At the time He thus entered upon the duties of His mission, He entered upon its penalties and pains. The cup of suffering which He filled to the brim, He afterwards drank to its dregs; and the cross which was placed upon His shoulders, He bore contentedly, till He planted it, as a tree of life, on the summit of Calvary. During the six long weeks of His sojourn in the wilderness, the absorption of His mind made Him independent of the body; and having fasted forty days, and forty nights, He was afterward an hungred. At this particular juncture, Satan assailed Him with a series of temptations, artfully concerted for the purpose of defeating His work.

The Temptation in the wilderness was designed to create distrust of the Father's goodness. "If thou be the Son of God," said the tempter, "command that these stones be made bread." It is probable the arch-fiend had either heard directly himself, or through some of his emissaries, the miraculous attestation of the Sonship of the Messiah, vouchsafed at His baptism. And now he approached Him to ascertain His identity, to sift His pretensions, and to overthrow by stratagem the glorious enterprise, which Christ came to accomplish. The question, with which he plied the Saviour, in this emergency, was plausibly and adroitly presented, implying that if He sustained so exalted a relationship to the Godhead, He had power to work a miracle on His own behalf, and that a fitting opportunity was now afforded to try that power, and prove His divinity. It was as if he had said, You are hungry and destitute, and yet the Son of God; demonstrate your right to the title, by converting these stones into bread, to satisfy your wants; speak the word, and spread for yourself a table in the wilderness, and thus place the matter beyond further dispute. There was no lack of art and subtilty in the mode of reasoning of the prince of darkness, who was endeavoring "to keep his goods in peace." Had it been complied with, it would have stopped the bread of heaven in its descent; and the world of hungry, starving souls would have been left to pine and perish. Whether the keen adversary came as an angel of light, "the aged man in rural weeds," or "the old man, his devotions singing," whom an early poet represents as "lowting low with prone obeisance and curtsey kind," the whole of his argument was such as might naturally be expected from a being of such intellect and wickedness, as the devil in disguise. But Jesus, with a majesty and authority that became His sacred character, rejected the counsel, and allowing the stones to remain stones, said, "It is written, Man shall not live by bread alone, but by every word that proceedeth out of the mouth of God." The foe was baffled by the artillery of Holy Writ, against which his machinations have ever been directed to impair its efficacy. The lowly Jesus could have foiled His assailant, with triumphant success, by drawing from the treasury of His own mind. There were resources within Himself, apart from the testimony of Scripture, sufficient to repel the dart, with a fearful rebound. But where, in that case, would have been our encouragement, when grappling with similar conflicts? How could we imitate His example, in the absence of such weapons to wield? The Saviour consulted the welfare of His people, in all that befell Him. The servant can now draw from the same armory as his Master, with the same favorable results. There is no temptation, but may be met and vanquished by the sword of the Spirit, which is the Word of God. The feeblest of the flock is invincible, when girded with truth. Does your "adversary, the devil, who goeth about as a roaring lion, seeking whom he may devour," suggest the staff of bread as the prime necessity? Does he propose the adoption of unchristian methods, in order to procure it? Does he insinuate doubts and suspicions of the Divine goodness and mercy? Suspect treachery in his whispers. Be not ignorant of his devices. Have recourse to the fountain of wisdom in the written word, till God shall bruise Satan under your feet, and comfort you with the fulness of His grace.

There are yearnings of the soul that can never be satisfied with bread alone,—capacities of the mind, which the finite cannot fill, and aspirations and claims which the world's provision fails to reach. There is an inner life, not visible to the eye, nor audible to the ear, nor apparent to the senses, the cravings of which demand that it should be nurtured with that higher and spiritual bread, which cometh down from heaven. The remonstrance, with which the Saviour bids us welcome to the bread, which feeds the soul, and the water, which allays its thirst, is, " Why spend ye money for that which is not bread, and your labor for that which satisfieth not? Hearken diligently unto me, and eat ye that which is good, and let your soul delight itself in fatness." The bread and water of life are the most precious things of heaven, and, by virtue of the mediation of Christ, are the freest and most accessible. They are like the rain-freighted clouds, which drop their fatness according to no geographical limits, but dispense their treasures to the needy of every land. And in whatever latitude and clime the inner life is thus sustained, it will develop its attributes, and flourish in prosperity, and adversity.

The Temptation, that assailed Christ from the pinnacle of the temple, was to daring presumption. "The devil taketh Him up into the Holy City, and setteth Him on a pinnacle of the temple, and saith unto Him, If thou be the Son of God, cast thyself down: for it is written, He shall give His angels charge concerning thee, and in their hands they shall bear thee up, lest at any time thou dash thy foot against a stone." The deceiver misquoted this passage from the Psalms, intentionally omitting the clause, "to keep thee in all thy ways," as unsuited to his purpose. The passage was cited by him, as a general promise of safety in *all* ways, whether of duty, or folly.

The sacred historian does not inform us, whether Christ was conveyed to the Holy City by supernatural means, or walked there of His own accord. Certainly there is no proof, that Satan had power to place Him there. The word translated, " taketh Him up," signifies no such thing. It simply means to conduct, to lead, to attend, to accompany, or, induce one to go. It is so employed in several places in the New Testament. " Jesus going up to Jerusalem, *took* the twelve disciples apart;" " And after six days, Jesus *taketh* Peter, James, and John." From these, and kindred texts, it would appear that Satan conducted, or accompanied Jesus to the pinnacle of the temple. The allusion is, probably, to that part of the temple, called Solomon's Porch. That sacred edifice was surrounded with porches and turrets, seventy-five feet in height. There was a pinnacle on the south side, that towered above the main body of the building a hundred and fifty feet.

From the top of this to the bottom of the valley below, exceeded the distance of seven hundred feet. It was doubtless on this dizzy eminence, that our Lord and Master stood. Satan also stood beside Him, and proposed that He should cast himself down. Was ever a proposition so wickedly audacious? And as if to render the descent the more certain, he alleged, that nothing could hurt Him; for the angels had been charged to bear Him gracefully up in their arms, and cause Him to alight softly. Need it be affirmed, how remote from the disposition of the Saviour would have been such a demonstration? "The kingdom of heaven cometh not with observation." Christ made no ostentatious display before a wondering people; and any feat of that sort, which pandered to the taste of the marvellous, would have been out of unison with the lowly ministry, upon which He was entering. With one volition, He could have commanded the attendance of more than twelve legions of angels, who hasten to do His will on earth, as they do it in heaven. But He wrought no miracles for

His own benefit, and was now contending with the enemy, in a manner, that should afford us an example, when plunged into perilous situations of exposure and trial.

The guardianship of angels is a solace to the children of sorrow, in the path of duty and perplexity, though it was never meant to extend to any persons, who trifle with the promised helps, by recklessness and presumption. Upon the proffered care of our heavenly Father we cannot rely too simply, or exclusively, when serving Him, in the way of His commandments; and we may confidently calculate on a glorious and triumphant result. But if the course we pursue lie not within the domain of truth, and Christian consistency, we only advance to a certain and ignoble defeat.

The most slippery steps of life are places of safety, when trodden in the providence of God. Those whom He calls into circumstances of trial and danger, He will interpose to protect. To the tempter He says, "Thus far shalt thou go, and no farther." Satan's power is limited. Had he possessed the ability to compel our Lord to cast Himself from the pinnacle of the temple, he would assuredly have done so, and not have suffered defeat. The want of power to accomplish his object, by coercion, still cleaves to him; and all he can do is, to entice, beguile, and delude; but not *compel*. Before he can succeed with his blandishments, he must have the consent of the human will. He may place you on the pinnacle of danger, he may carry you to the extreme verge of the precipice, he may discourse with flattering breath, and conjure up to your imagination scenes of ecstasy and bliss; but this is the limit of his range. The heart, uplifted to heaven, is girded with the strength of resistance. The look to the sympathizing Saviour turns the tide of battle, and insures the victory.

The third Temptation, brought to bear upon our blessed Lord, was to gross and wicked idolatry. He is transferred from the pinnacle of the temple, to the top of an exceeding high mountain. What mountain, we are not informed. It was, probably, one of the most elevated in the vicinity of Jerusalem, from the summit of which could be seen no small part of the land of Israel. The prophet Moses, before his death, was commanded to go up to the top of Mount Nebo, and God showed him "all the land of Gilead unto Dan, and all Naphtali, and the land of Ephraim, and Manasseh, and all the land of Judah unto the utmost sea, and the south, and the plain of the valley of Jericho, and the city of palm-trees unto Zoar." Whether the prince of the power of the air selected Nebo, or Mount Tabor, from which to open up the vision of unbounded scenery is quite immaterial. The latitude allowed by the literal interpretation of the words of the inspired historian, would lead us to the conclusion, that it was a mountain of great eminence, commanding an extensive prospect, where the evil one made to pass before the eye of Christ an exhibition of "all the kingdoms of the world, and the glory of them." All were spread out in their extent and proportion; in their flower and beauty; in their pride and glory. Mountain and plain, river and valley, city and villa, schools of wisdom, and laurels of fame; imperial saloons and sumptuous banquets; all that was beautiful in Nature and magnificent in Art; all that the eye covets or the imagination conceives; all the perishable joys of earth were brought forth in their most glowing colors, dazzling with the bright and sparkling hues, that sparkle over them. The picture was drawn with a masterly hand, and presented to Christ as a gorgeous scene. All these are mine, said the tempter, and "all these will I give thee, if thou wilt fall down and worship me." Oh, the horrible audacity of that fallen spirit! Who but the incarnate Son of the Eternal, could escape from such a fiery trial, untainted by the ebullition of indignant passion? The meekest saint upon earth would have been tempted to speak unadvisedly with his lips. That monstrous proposal was a bolder attack than any that had been offered. It was a deadly thrust at the Saviour's divinity. The Son of God worship the devil? Was ever wickedness so unexampled? "Get thee behind me, Satan," fell like a thunderbolt on his guilty head; "for it is written, thou shalt worship the

Lord thy God, and Him only shalt thou serve." If the old serpent had any doubts before of the Godhead of Christ, he had none now. And like a storm-cloud, driven away by the wind, "the devil left Him, and behold angels came and ministered unto Him." Once more the Holy Jesus found himself in a calm, restored to His native element, and surrounded with affectionate intelligences, who ever worship before Him.

The proffered bribe, "all these will I give thee," is still the bait by which the deceiver acquires, one by one, through all time, and all generations, his countless devotees. Around and about us, he is industriously engaged, in holding forth the same temptations and false allurements. The wealth and vanity of the world are the gilded toys, by which he seeks to dazzle the vision, and to win the heart. But these, his brightest gifts, are an empty pageant, a deceitful show. Nor does the world really belong to him. He holds only a fraudulent occupancy, in a few dark corners of it. "The earth is the Lord's, and the fulness thereof."

He created it, and furnished it with life, and the means of happiness. He upholds it by the word of His power. His title to it, as Proprietor, is perfect, and His right to its actual possession, and to all its revenue, equally incontestable. Never has He ceased to assert the validity of His claim, and to signify His intention of prosecuting it upon a plan that is preëminently His own, until it shall have been fully honored, in the reclamation of His plundered premises.

The Spirit, and the Word of God are effective agencies, in overcoming the wiles of the devil. It was in the fulness of the Spirit, that Christ entered the contest of grappling with the adversary, and from the armory of the Spirit, drew the weapon that put him to flight. We are thus taught by His example, to live in the Spirit, to walk in the Spirit, and to repose our defence on the moral influence of the sword of the Spirit, upon our choice and conduct. There is enough in the written Word, when employed in humble dependence on the Holy Spirit's aid, to carry us through every conflict, and make us "more than conquerors, through Him that loved us." The naked promise of the Spirit, apart from the Word, through which He usually operates, is not enough; nor must we expect that He will make use of this instrument on our behalf, unless we are found diligently employing its prescriptions, in the way of His requirements.

Our daily life is one continued warfare, in which there can be no truce, no compromise, and no exemption. "We wrestle not against flesh and blood, but against principalities, against powers, against the rulers of the darkness of this world, against spiritual wickedness in high places." We contend with the several ranks of satanic influence, invisible and impalpable, whom success has made bold, and experience sagacious. Every inch we yield, the enemy gains; and every inch he gains, is an encouragement to gain still more. Boldly must we resist the tramp of his malignant fury, and vigorously continue the warfare, till death proclaims the deliverance and the victory.

## THE THREE MARYS AT THE CROSS.

It was a bright and beautiful day, when the Son of the Highest travelled to the scene of death. The birds carolled in the trees. The fields were clothed in the gayety of spring attire. The flowers loaded the air with fragrance. The breeze whispered nothing but love. All evinced tokens of rejoicing, save Jesus and his sorrowing friends. The multitude that formed the procession was a mixed one, consisting of all sorts and conditions of men. Spears, and helmets, and drawn swords, glittered in the sunshine. Soldiers on foot, and on horses. Scribes and Pharisees, Jews and Gentiles, high and low, blended together in the crowd. Some were following in the train, whose sick ones Christ had healed, whose wounded hearts He had comforted, and on whose pathway of darkness He had shed the light of heaven. They lifted up their voices in sympathy with His sufferings and wept. The Lord of Glory turned to them and said, " Weep not for me, but weep for yourselves and your children." His all-prescient eye could discern in the distance the dreadful malediction, which the infuriated populace were bringing down upon themselves, in the form of a foreign invasion, which would lay in ruins both their city and temple.

The hill-top is reached. Now mark what takes place on that eminence. Rude and brutal men offer the Holy One of Israel a stupefying potion. But He disdains the draught, choosing to submit to the will of His Father in the full consciousness of His faculties. They proceed to tear the clothes from His sacred body, and leave Him only His crown of thorns. They lay Him down on the wood, on which He is to bleed. They stretch His arms along the timber, with the palms of the hands upturned. They take the hammer, and iron spikes, and lo ! there is a silence pervading the crowd, — a deep, solemn, profound silence, similar to that which is felt in the house of mourning, when the coffin is screwed down. The silence is broken, and there is heard blow after blow through the quivering tendons of that sacred frame. How harshly they thunder upon the ear, testifying in horrible language the demerit of sin. But, blessed be God, there is mercy in the severest dispensation. There is light behind the darkest cloud. Those nails pierced the handwriting that was against us, and fulfilled the prediction of the Psalmist, "They pierced my hands, and my feet." And those pierced hands, and bleeding feet are the source of our greatest blessings. They are the wounded members of an Almighty Saviour, who loved us, and gave Himself for us.

The cross is raised erect, and jerked into the ground. The Saviour is lifted up from the earth, to draw all men unto Him. The place of torture is bedewed with a crimson stream that works marvels. The Lion of the tribe of Judah bleeds, that He may overthrow and conquer. He consents to be clothed with ignomy, that He might beget our liberty. He empties the cup of wrath, that He might fill it with blessings.

In the outskirts of the assembled throng there is an estimable little group, that meets the eye like a benignant constellation in the darkness of night. They are a band of pious women, distressed mourners, viewing afar off. But the cords of love are drawing them to the cross. Love, strong as death, is impelling them onward. They are pushing their way through the sons of Belial, to be close on the spot. Earth has but few charms for them now. It is a thorny and thirsty soil, where the flowers of Paradise bloom only to wither. They had embarked their all in the Crucified One, and are anxious to show their heartfelt sympathy and veneration for the sufferer. Of the world's contumely and scorn they have no dread. The weak maintain their ground, while the strong have fled. The timid conquer, while the heroes despair. And now these faithful souls stand by the cross, the personification of love, which many waters cannot quench, nor the floods drown.

We recognize in the group, the most blessed among women, the sorely tried mother of our

Lord, in whom Simeon's prophecy is fulfilled, "A sword shall pierce through thine own soul also." She had probably no presentiment that it would be accomplished in this manner. Yet she stands, with tottering steps, to see the end. She beholds the drooping head, the brow wrung with anguish, and the quivering lip. She sees the warm blood gushing, and hears the cry of His distress, under the hidings of His heavenly Father's countenance. Though she can offer no relief, her maternal solicitude will not permit her to withdraw from the spot. The gold is in the crucible, and the Refiner himself is at hand, alleviating and adjusting the trial to the burdened heart. Her Son dies, with all the earthly connection, in which she had hitherto stood in relation to Him. But she views Him by faith as the Lord and Prince of a kingdom, which shall never be moved. She looks upon the infant of days as the Ancient of days,—the Light of the world as sustaining an eclipse,—the Sun of Righteousness as setting in the shades of death, to rise in glory, as the Resurrection and the Life. The words that He had spoken unto her respecting the necessity of His sufferings, and the glory that should follow, now caused her to realize more fully the spirit and meaning of her own splendid *Magnificat*, "My soul doth magnify the Lord, and my spirit hath rejoiced in God, my Saviour. For He hath regarded the low estate of His handmaiden: for behold, from henceforth all generations shall call me blessed. For He that is mighty hath magnified me, and holy is His name. And His mercy is on them that fear Him throughout all generations."

Of the richness and fulness of His mercy, He had just given a most convincing demonstration, in His regard to the repentant malefactor, who was expiring at His side. And is it presumption to hope, that, in the sublime situation which He occupies on the cross, He will condescend to notice His mother, and open His gracious lips to give her one parting word? The eye of His love has not yet ceased to rest on her. She has still a place in His heart, amid the cares of the world's redemption. With a look of sublime tranquillity, peculiar only to

Himself, He points her to the disciple whom He loved, and says, "Woman, behold thy Son;" and to John, He says, "Behold thy mother." Those blessed accents carried balm to the wounded heart. The tones of that familiar voice, and the peaceful expression of His eye were as if He said, Mother, I leave you, but I only go to my Father's happy abode " to prepare a place for you; and if I go and prepare a place for you, I will come again and receive you unto myself, that where I am, there ye may be also." In the mean while I commit you to the care of John, who will cheer your mournful hours, and become your support and solace. Give him my place, as a son, in your holy love; and his whole soul will repay the confidence reposed in him, as he calls you mother. From that hour, that disciple took her unto his own home. Joseph, her husband, had fallen asleep, and John thenceforth took her under his special care and protection, happy to possess in her an object, toward whom he could manifest the gratitude and affection he felt for his Lord. It may seem strange that the

Saviour, in speaking to Mary, should have made use of the cold and distant word "Woman." But the form of address was common, and perfectly respectful. The word in ancient Greek is equivalent to Lady, and in Hebrew to Mistress. And as He was just preparing to ascend to the throne of the Eternal Majesty, as King of kings, and Lord of lords, He endeavored to elevate her mind above the sphere of merely human conception, to that infinitely higher region, where all earthly relations are merged into the spiritual. He was henceforth to be her priest, and Lord, and she was to honor and adore Him as one of His daughters. The mode of expression was therefore not likely to wound her already bleeding heart, by exciting unnecessarily a storm of human emotion, which the word mother, would be apt to produce. It also saved her from exposure to the rudeness of the surrounding rabble. Mother, brother, and sister, are designations applicable to all who love our Lord Jesus Christ in sincerity and in truth. "Who is my mother, and who are my brethren?" said Christ. And stretching forth His hand toward His disciples, He said, "Behold my mother, and my brethren! For whosoever shall do the will of my Father who is in heaven, the same is my mother, and sister, and brother."

The next time we hear of the Virgin Mary was on the occasion of the disciples' return from Mount Olivet, after the Ascension. She met with them, in the large upper-room at Jerusalem, and united with the company in pouring out her soul in prayer to her ascended Lord. This is the last account we have of her in the New Testament. If she survived any lengthened period, she, probably, accompanied the Apostle John, when he went to reside at Ephesus, though it is more reasonable to conclude that the Great Head of the Church, foreseeing the difficulties that were gathering upon the Jews, took her from the evil to come. "Blessed art thou among women," is the appropriate epitaph, which every Christian would have inscribed on her tomb.

There were two other Marys at the Crucifixion, whom the Evangelist particularly mentions.

"Now there stood by the cross of Jesus His mother, and His mother's sister, Mary the wife of Cleophas, and Mary Magdalene." St. John mentions Mary the wife of Cleophas as the sister, or relative of the Virgin. Her husband was also called Alpheus, and was the father, as this Mary was the mother, of James; and Joses, and Simon, and Judas, who are therefore called the brethren, or kinsmen of our Lord. She had the pleasure of seeing her children received into the fellowship of the great Shepherd, and usefully employed in His church. James was for many years Pastor in Jerusalem, and was indefatigably engaged in the discharge of his sacred duties, when Saul visited the Metropolis, after his conversion. He also presided in a general council, held in the year of our Lord 61, and was successful in controlling its decision. He was the writer of the Epistle that bears his name,— a rich legacy to the Church, by which he, being dead, yet speaketh. These brethren of our Lord may have been scattered with the rest of the flock, when the sword fell upon the Shepherd; but their excellent mother felt it her paramount duty to appear at the cross in their absence, and by her own fidelity and cheerful service to cover their flight.

And lo! there is Mary Magdalene sobbing aloud, overwhelmed with grief, ready to die for her Lord. She had experienced His delivering power from a complication of maladies that afflicted her. She had followed Him from place to place, to minister to Him of her substance. She attended Him in His last journey from Galilee to Jerusalem. And she is now at the foot of the cross, with His mother, and His mother's sister, Mary the wife of Cleophas. These faithful souls were not present with any view to His rescue; but to show their sympathy, to observe His behavior, to hear His dying expressions, and to declare their steadfast adherence to Him as devoted followers. They cling to Him, with their love and hope, like ivy to a fallen tree. Christ had been made of God unto them wisdom, righteousness, sanctification, and redemption. He had blessed them with all spiritual blessings, in heavenly places. He was their life — their all. The signs extraordinary, which they have just witnessed, — the darkness, the rending rocks, and the quivering earth, — are attestations of His divinity, that swell like a favorable gale the sails of their hope afresh, and encourage them to hold fast their confidence, which hath great recompence of reward.

The Saviour has yielded up the ghost. Death has spread his sable wings over the sufferers. The gazing spectators have dispersed to their homes. The winds of angry passion have subsided to a calm. Solemn stillness broods over the scene, like a placid evening after the turmoil of a tempestuous day. The season of preparation has arrived, and the Sabbath is drawing on. Two honorable men, Joseph of Arimathea, and Nicodemus, who came to Jesus by night, are intrusted with the interment of the corpse. They have obtained permission from the Governor to commence their mournful labors. They fetch and plant a ladder against the cross of the Prince of Peace, whose head has fallen over upon His breast. As they proceed to ascend it, with reverential awe, they feel as if they were mounting the steps of some sacred temple. Their minds are deeply affected as they gaze on the lofty majesty that sits enthroned on that pallid brow. They can scarcely help thinking of what may yet come to pass before three suns shall rise and set. Tenderly and softly they draw the nails from His hands and feet. The precious corpse reclines upon their shoulders, and they let it gently to the ground. Quietly it is conveyed to the grave, without pomp or ceremony, attended by the weeping Marys, and other courageous females, who are anxious to see the place where His remains are deposited. They at once tender their services, — wash the blood from His sacred temples, and then return to prepare spices and ointments. If Mary, the sister of Lazarus, were there, she would remember the anointing which He received at her hands in Bethany, and which He declared was for the day of his burial. The inanimate treasure is deposited in a rocky sepulchre in Joseph's garden. The sun is casting his last rays upon it, and the evening twilight its cool shades. In this peaceful seclusion the Holy One is to find His earthly resting-place, till the predicted morn shall witness Him bursting the barriers of the tomb as death's conqueror. His burial service was chanted by the prophet Isaiah many centuries before. " And He made His grave with the wicked, and with the rich in his death; because He had done no violence, neither was guile found in His mouth."

Early on Sunday morning, while it was yet dark, the Marys were at the sepulchre, which they found vacated. The Lord had risen, and become the first-fruits of them that slept. The Easter dawn broke in beauty and blessing, giving the oil of joy for mourning, and the garment of praise for the spirit of heaviness. Likewise should we reckon ourselves also to be dead into sin, but alive unto God, through Jesus Christ our Lord. " If we be planted in the likeness of His death, we shall be also in the likeness of His resurrection."

The lesson inculcated by the position which the three Marys occupied at the Crucifixion is that the road to enduring happiness lies by the way of the cross. The wondrous cross is full of blessings, — vast as the mind that procured them, vast as the heart that bestows them. View it in its offer of peace and pardon, bought with blood. Bring to it body and spirit, as a willing sacrifice. Fling away all doubt. Renounce all claim. Draw near to it with a confiding, loving, trusting heart, and say to Him who bled on it, —

> "In my hand no price I bring;
> Simply to Thy cross I cling."

Cling to it with an unyielding grasp. Clasp it with arms that the world shall never unlock. Live upon it the life of godliness. Cherish it in the matter of your salvation, the power of God. Jesus died, is our life. Jesus reigns, is our strength. Our trust is on His sacrifice. Our hope is on His crown. The creation of life comes from the one. The continuance of life flows from the other. The starting-place for heaven is at the foot of the cross. Only as we feel our need of the sacrifice of Jesus, and wash in the fountain of His blood, can we ever be prepared for the mansions of purity and rest. Do we resort to another refuge? It is a refuge of lies. Do we build on another foundation? It is a foundation of sand. Do we cherish another hope? It is a hope that will perish. Thousands of rams, and ten thousands of rivers of oil; the gift of the first-born for the transgressions, the fruit of the body for the sin of the soul, can perform nothing in advancing toward the prize of eternity. The record still stands. "There is none other name under heaven, given among men, whereby we must be saved." Over all other prospects there hangs the gathering gloom of condemnation and despair. When you think of the hour of your departure, remember that your only rescue from the grasp of the destroyer, and your only happiness in finding death transformed into a messenger of mercy, is that you have stood by the cross, as one crucified with Christ. When you think of the scenery of the judgment, forget not that you can only attain to the station of acceptance and blessedness, as you inhale the atmosphere of Calvary, and are one with Him who bled and died. And when you think of the world of light and blessedness beyond the shadows of the sepulchre, and gaze upon the multitude of the redeemed in the high state of their rejoicing, we remind you that the crown was gained by the cross, and that there is no heaven, but through the blood of the Lamb. We may form imaginations of heaven, but apart from this, they are all vain and theoretical. They are as delusive as if we were to lie down and dream of scenes of magnificence and beauty, — vast and splendid palaces, — a serene and cloudless sky, and the fair earth imaging forth a paradise of verdure and grandeur; and there we revel in ectasy and delight. But the morning comes. It was but a baseless fiction; and it is gone. And so he who thinks of heaven, without connecting his thoughts with the work of the cross, is but dreaming; and if he wake not to a proper consciousness in time, he will awake when it is too late, and discover that he has lost the heaven on which he dreamt in vain.

# THE THREE DYING WORDS OF CHRIST.

> " Hark! the voice of love and mercy
> Sounds aloud from Calvary;
> See! it rends the rocks asunder,
> Shakes the earth, and veils the sky
> 'It is finished!'
> Hear the dying Saviour cry."

THE last words of persons are unusually impressive. They chime upon the ear like intelligence from another world, and produce a more abiding effect on the hearts of survivors. The last words of Jesus, as he hung upon the cross, are preëminently important. We are wont to apprehend in them a meaning and an emphasis, which no reach of mind can fully grasp, and no power of language fitly express. There was much in the creative word, that rolled forth in immensity, and called a world into existence, and said, "Let there be light, and there was light." There was much of awe and astonishment in the legislative voice that pealed from Sinai, when the mountain shook, and the multitude of Israel did exceedingly fear and quake. But we are more struck with the significancy of the Redeemer's cry that sounded from Calvary, "It is finished," when He bowed His head, and gave up the ghost. It was not the moan of the breaking heart; it was not the shriek of the writhing frame; it was not the wail of sinking hope. It was the cry of satisfaction, the shout of victory, the burst of triumph. It was heard by the confounded disciples, and weeping females, who had followed Him from Galilee; heard by Herod the tetrarch, and Pilate the governor, and their courtiers and men of war; heard by the Scribes, and the Pharisees, and the bigoted elders, and the great council of the Jewish nation. It was heard by the thousands then assembled at the Feast, who had so recently shouted, "Away with him; crucify him." It was heard in heaven; and there was silence, in the region of perpetual song. It was heard in hell, and there ensued a pause, in the howl of malevolence, and in the groan of despair. The earth upheaved in convulsive pang; the bright sky folded itself in blackest gloom; the globe was stirred through all its zones. It was the hour of conquest over the powers of darkness; the hour to which all the past had looked forward, and on which all the future hung; the hour when Christ's right hand and holy arm had gotten Him the victory. There were but few among the conspirators of that vast concourse, who were willing to acknowledge these glorious achievements. The god of this world had so blinded their eyes, that they were ignorant of the fallacy of their own schemes. Even the poor disciples, though they had often been instructed in these matters, were destitute of any clear perceptions. They continued, until after His resurrection, fools, and slow of heart to believe all that the prophets had spoken. In the discussion of a theme of such vital importance, it will be proper to set forth some of those things, touching the cross, that are assuredly believed by us, and that will be dear to our hearts forever; things for which the Saviour became incarnate, and in reference to which He could say, " O, righteous Father, I have glorified Thee on the earth: I have finished the work, which Thou gavest me to do." The work was finished on Calvary, for which He came forth from the excellent glory, and to which He had devoted His mortal life.

The purposes of God were finished in the manifestation of His character. He had proposed to Himself a revenue of glory from an assemblage of excellent and happy beings that should brighten through eternity. Their excellency and happiness were made to depend; not upon any arbitrary constitution of the divine government, but upon their harmony with His spirit, and obedience to His laws. This harmony and obedience, we should suppose, might be produced by motives appealing to love, or motives appealing to fear; displays of benevolence, or displays of justice. The former would seem all-sufficient, had it not been proved ineffectual by the revolt of angels, and the apostasy of man. And the latter, while it might engender slavish fear, could never induce that generous exultation in the service of God, with which He would be pleased, or honored. It was now requisite that there should be a *new* exhibition of Deity. Not an exhibition of *mercy only;* for that would be tantamount to the abrogation of the law. But an exhibition in which, if it were possible, the motives to love, and the motives to fear might go hand in hand; an exhibition that should take away none of God's attractiveness, nor strip sin of any of its deformity; that should render the Divine Goodness yet more affecting, and the Divine Justice yet more august; which should throw a more frightful repellancy around the forms of evil, and a greater adorableness around the majesty of heaven. Such an admirable exhibition is tendered us in the propitiatory sacrifice of the Son of God. The Lord of Life stoops to a death of ignomy, to cancel the guilt of His murderers. The Teacher of heaven, for whom Socrates had taught himself and his scholars to hope, and whom all Judea admired, gives His lessons on the cross. The King of Glory blends the lowest condescension with the loftiest splendor, and endures the treatment due to consummate wickedness. Behold Him, laden with our iniquity, and burdened with our sins!

Behold Him in the convulsion of an agony that presses the blood from every pore! Look at Him in this voluntary act of humiliation and suffering, and say, whether the character and government of God are not associated with grace and mercy to an extent never before known. Ideas so enlarged and accurate could not have been obtained from any other source. The heavens had declared the glory of God, and the firmament showed His handiwork. The earth, the stars, and all their tenantry proclaimed, in tones of sublimity and sweetness, His unfathomable mind,—His wonder-working arm. But it was on the cross that He gave us the best and fullest manifestation of himself. Here we gaze upon Him full-orbed, with all His round of rays complete. Here we see the love of God, in giving us His Son; the mercy of God, announcing to us the exceeding riches of His grace; the justice and holiness of God, in their most stern requirements; all the perfections of God in beautiful harmony. Here mercy and truth meet together: righteousness and peace embrace each other.

We recognize in Christ the Father's representative, whose mission was to make Him known; to unfold His attributes; to explain His law; to pour forth the ocean of His love, and to work out an everlasting righteousness, which shall be unto all, and upon all them that believe. As we look into His Godlike countenance, afresh, the declaration seems to fall upon our ears, "He that hath seen me, hath seen the Father." We see in the Saviour all that is to be seen of the Godhead; and we regard His finished work as the stability, the perfection, and the blessing of our race. Take away the divinity of Christ, and there has been no satisfaction to justice, and no sacrifice for sin. Seal up the fountain of Christ's precious blood, and you seal up the soul to blackness, darkness, and despair. Deny the efficacy of the Atonement, and there is nothing more left to hope for; the present becomes all recklessness, and the future all hopelessness, and the thousands and tens of thousands of our fellow-beings, like mariners tossed upon the wide ocean, without a compass or a star.

When Christ said, "It is finished," He had reference to the issue of that conflict with Satan, which had been carried on from the Fall. At an early period the old serpent was permitted to harass and vex our race, to declare war with the seed of the woman, and to introduce sin and misery into the beautiful world, which the Creator had pronounced very good. He came with all the phantoms of delusion, and all the sorceries of vice, to ensnare and beguile. He came to establish himself upon his despot throne, and to erect a monarchy, within which to gather the nations of the earth, who were hateful, and hating one another. On the part of God, there appeared to be no direct effective opposition for many ages, and Satan seemed to reign and rule without interruption. The strong man armed kept his palace and goods in peace. Darkness indeed covered the earth, and gross darkness the people. The evil one could well boast himself the god of this world. He was the ruler of its darkness, the wickedness of its high places, the spirit of its legislation, and its public sway. In him the children of disobedience appeared to live, and move, and have their being. The time had at length arrived, when his kingdom began to depart from him, and Satan was seen falling as lightning from heaven. The woman's seed had come into notice, who should bruise his head. The dread Avenger, beneath whose arm he had sunk to the deep abyss, was now incarnate as the champion of man. The fiend, aware of the peril approaching his kingdom, began to marshal up all his force, and to prepare for the contest with deadly hostility. While yet the mighty babe was folded to His mother's breast, he assailed Him with the assassin knife. Then he proceeded to test His virtue by the seduction of pleasure and power; then to try His patience; then to deprive Him of His life. At last he had the ghastly satisfaction of seeing the Jew and the Gentile nail the Lord of life and glory to the tree. Now he imagined all was over with his adversary, and was ready to exclaim, "I have overcome thee, O thou Galilean." He began to mock the Ruler of the skies. He had bruised the heel, the mortality, the outer man of Christ. But he had not touched the *head,* the *spirit,* the *immortal,* the Divine nature. The demon's triumph was premature. He was taken in his own craftiness; was the instrument of his own defeat. Through his wily machinations the determinate counsel and foreknowledge of God were fulfilled. The tide of battle turned against him, and he was made a show of openly. The principle was fully developed before which he must flee. The elements of moral agency were brought out of darkness into marvellous light. The rays of truth, that had been scattered over past generations, were gathered as in a focus, to advance "from conquering to conquer." Calvary became the centre, from which the power of victory proceeded to the east and to the west, to the north and to the south, to find no limits but the uttermost ends of the earth, and no date, but the close of time. Ever since the epoch in question, there has been a gradual breaking up, and breaking down of those systems, by which the spirit of evil has held the governance of man. One after another his Dagons have fallen, his oracles have fled, his plans proved abortive.

Every revolution among the nations has left him weakened in his defences, and impaired in his resources. Every rolling year has witnessed, more and more, the emancipation of his subjects into the glorious liberty of the sons of God. Yet a little while, and there shall be heard a great voice of much people in heaven, saying, Alleluia: and it shall be answered by the voice of earth, delivered from its groaning bondage, as it were "the voice of a great multitude, and as the voice of many waters, and as the voice of many thunderings, saying Alleluia: for the Lord God omnipotent reigneth." In that voice we shall recognize the full meaning of the Saviour's cry, when He bowed His head and gave up the ghost.

The death of Jesus finished the types and shadows of the old economy. Its institutions were all so constituted as to prefigure Christ and His sufferings. If beasts were slain, and victims bled, they pointed to Him and His intercession. But when the cross was set up, and the holy Jesus was suspended on it, the types and shadows instantly retired, leaving all the glory to Him, who is the end of the law for righteousness to every one that believeth. The fires that burned on Jewish altars were now extinguished to be lit no more. The clouds of incense that sent up their perfumes were done away. Legal sacrifices were brought to a perpetual end. The Lord required no more the reeking of the blood of shuddering victims. The paschal lamb, the daily oblation, the sin-offering, the scape-goat, all received their consummation in the death of the Lamb slain, from the foundation of the world. The rending of the vail of the temple, from the top to the bottom, proclaimed that "Christ entered, not into the holy place made with hands, but into heaven itself, there to appear in the presence of God for us." "Almost all things in the law were purged with blood, and without shedding of blood there was no remission." "If the blood of bulls and goats, and the ashes of an heifer, sprinkling the unclean, sanctifieth to the purifying of the flesh, how much more shall the blood of Christ, who through the Eternal Spirit offered Himself without spot unto God, purify your consciences from dead works to serve the living God." "We are redeemed, not with corruptible things, such as silver and gold, but with the precious blood of Christ, as of a lamb without blemish, and without spot." "We have redemption through His blood, even the forgiveness of sin." The blood of the immaculate Jesus flowed from the arteries of a spotless humanity, upon which not a breath of pollution had fallen. This satisfied the claims of injured Justice, honored the Divine perfections, placed the Church on an immovable basis, and "opened the kingdom of heaven to all believers." O, could we have looked up to Him at that eventful moment, — could we have witnessed the suffering Saviour pardon the thief, and breathe out His soul in supplication for His murderers, — could we have heard the Redeemer's last cry, "It is finished," and have noticed the sensation which the wonders accompanying it everywhere produced, — we should have felt that we were listening to a Being possessed of the sovereign and uncircumscribed energy of the universe, comprising in Himself limitation and infinity, absolute dominion, and entire resignation.

The finished work of Christ made the cross the medium of all our blessings. Pent up and restrained by the wickedness of men, they found vent on Calvary, and burst forth in a flood of healing mercy to irrigate our souls. The resources of infinite love had all been deposited in the hands of Christ, to be communicated through the cross. The cross and the Saviour's blessings are never separated. The manifold temporal, spiritual, and eternal enjoyments that were vouchsafed for four thousand years before Christ was crucified; all that have been received since; and all that will hereafter be bestowed, till the consummation of all things; all the deliverances from coming wrath, and all the oceans of joy in heaven,— all flow from the cross. The cross is the channel of Divine affluence, the centre of the strongest attachment, the bond of the closest union, the shrine at which the world shall worship, the eminence from which the Christian shall ascend to his final rest. We owe everything to the cross,— redemption from iniquity, exemption from condemnation, adoption into God's family, the witness of the Spirit, heirship with Christ, and a title to glory. The cross softens into penitence, mellows into gratitude, ravishes with delight, and infuses into the bosom the germ of a new life. Have we wandered from God? here we are brought back. Were we shut out from the kingdom of heaven? here the door of admission is thrown open. Are we terrified at the approach of death? we are enabled to overcome through the blood of the Lamb. Rally round the cross; think much of the cross; speak of the wonders of the cross; pray "God forbid that I should glory, save in the cross of Jesus Christ my Lord."

It was finished when Christ died, with His personal humiliation and suffering. The miseries of this life, which fell upon Him in every variety, and form, and degree, completed their cycle with His expiring breath. The bitter cup, which was given Him to drink, was drained of its last dregs. Poverty and persecution ceased to attend Him as companions. The sufferer was king upon the cross, and held His life till the Scriptures were accomplished. He had power over His own life, power to retain it, power to lay it down, and power to take it again. The loud voice, with which He gave up the ghost, asserted His supremacy as Lord and Master over nature, and His perfect independence of the injustice of His foes. It showed that He died not from mere exhaustion, as was the case with the thieves who were crucified with Him. Instead of losing His voice, as the dying usually do, so that he who attends the death-bed can only hear soft whispers, Jesus *cried aloud*, as if bidding death approach Him. "The Lord shall go forth as a mighty man," saith the prophet. "He shall stir up jealousy like a man of war. He shall cry, yea roar, yea prevail against His enemies." The loud dying cry is a demonstrative evidence that the crucified Saviour did not die from necessity, but of His own free will; not from weakness, but from choice. Freely admit this precious truth, and it takes away all that shame and reproach from His sufferings, which His enemies are wont to cast on them, and converts them into a pure and voluntary oblation. It changes the cross of infamy into the sign of renown, and the crown of thorns into the many crowns of earth, and heaven, and all the stars. The adorable Redeemer was now Head over all things to His Church; Lord of angels and men, exalted far above all principality and power, and might and dominion. His hands were on the reins of universal empire, and all worlds were prepared to lay their diadems at His feet. Have we loyal and loving hearts? Do we yield obedience to His righteous laws? Then we shall acknowledge the kingdom to be His, and His forever. We shall pray, Reign blessed Saviour in our hearts; reign in our homes; reign in our land; reign in our world. Thine is the kingdom, and the power, and the glory. Thou art worthy to receive blessing, and honor, and glory, and power. Thou art worthy,— Thou alone.

The contemplation of a theme so interesting and delightful should put an end to all our misgivings, apathy, and indifference. The propitiatory sacrifice of the Son of God was the most wonderful event that ever occurred in the annals of time; and there will be none more wonderful in the annals of eternity. Then, shall it not arrest your thought? Shall it not excite your study? Shall it not fill you with sweet and sublime inspiration? Shall the world, or friends, or enemies, — shall anything interfere to prevent your giving it the warmest place in your affections? Oh, shame on that sensualism, which precludes from a theme so pure. Shame on that worldliness, which precludes from a theme so high. Shame on that debasement, which precludes from communion with the very heart of God. Awake, awake, from the petty concerns that occupy your attention from day to day. Arouse, arouse, from the paltry interests that engross and agitate your minds from week to week. Fix your contemplation on Calvary. Bring your thought and feeling to the cross. Be fearful lest you lose sight of its glory. Keep it in full view. Do everything in the light that beams from it. Hearken to the cry, "It is finished." Dwell upon its meaning, as it bears on the character of God, and your future destiny. Pray that you may know Christ. Pray that you may be crucified with Christ; pray that your life may be hidden with Christ in God; and when "Christ, who is your life, shall appear, then shall you also appear with Him in glory." But alas! many there are who refuse to look at the cross. How will you escape if you neglect so great a salvation? How? We beseech you, tell us. How will you answer the Saviour, who died that you might live? How will you answer Him, when He shall come in the glory of His Father, and of His holy angels? How will you answer for the neglect of His gospel in that great and terrible day? "Kiss the Son lest He be angry, and you perish from the way, when His wrath is kindled but little." "Blessed are all they that put their trust in Him."

It should be finished with all our unbelief. It is unbelief that dishonors the Saviour, and ties up His hands so that He cannot bless us while we continue in that state. He could not do many mighty works among His countrymen, because of their unbelief. "He that cometh to God, must believe that He is, and that He is the rewarder of them that diligently seek Him."

The Jews could not enter Canaan on account of their unbelief. "And the fearful and the unbelieving shall have their part in the lake that burneth with fire and brimstone, which is the second death." Yet, in the very face of the most solemn facts and denunciations, we discover around us the most palpable proofs of the prevalence of unbelief: persons who profess to believe in Christ, and are dead in trespasses and in sins; believers, and yet unbelievers; nominally receiving the Saviour, yet really rejecting Him; consenting to Him, and yet denying Him; vindicating Him, and yet turning away from Him; assenting to Him in the judgment, yet refusing Him in the heart. Throw off, we beseech you, such anomalies, and be Christians in deed and in truth. "For he is not a Jew who is one outwardly; neither is that circumcision which is outward in the flesh; but he is a Jew who is one inwardly, and circumcision is that of the heart; in the spirit, and not in the letter; whose praise is not of men, but of God."

It will soon be finished with this mortal life.

We shall soon look upon each other for the last time. We shall soon pass, not merely from this particular spot, but from this world altogether. We shall soon stand before the presence of the Eternal. It will then be finished with all our happiness, or with all our misery. We shall then mingle with the joys of the blessed, or wail with the shrieks of the lost. We shall have before us a long and glorious eternity, or an accursed immortality. Which shall it be? Shall we dwell in heaven, or in hell? Shall we inherit with Christ and the glorified, or with the devil and his angels? Gracious and loving God, merciful and precious Saviour, holy and powerful Spirit, grant us an inheritance among all them that are sanctified.

## THE THREE ASCENSIONS.

EACH of the three grand dispensations of religion has alike been favored with a remarkable instance of translation into heaven: the patriarchal, in the person of Enoch; the Jewish, in the person of Elijah; and the Christian, in the person of Christ. These are beautiful exceptions to those who have died in the Lord, — bright lights that illumine the darkness of the sepulchre, and which assure us of a pathway to a state of felicity and glory far beyond.

Upwards of three hundred years Enoch was contemporary with Adam, and must have learned from his intercourse with the father of our race the history of Creation, — the circumstances of the Fall; the terms of the Promise; and much that pertained to the wisdom, rectitude, and goodness of the Divine administration. The knowledge, thus acquired, had a happy influence in shaping his private and public life. At a time when the rest of mankind were mostly living in open rebellion against the Majesty of Heaven, and provoking the vengeance of the Almighty with their ungodly deeds, he walked with God, and obtained the exalted testimony that "he pleased God." This was the sublime feature in his history, — the leading touch in the picture that revealed all the rest. Like the great law of gravitation in the physical world, the closeness of his walk with God kept the other parts of his life in beautiful proportion and harmony.

But what strikes us so forcibly in the account of one so eminent, is the little that is said of him. The whole of his memoir is comprised in one solitary paragraph. We see his biography and epitaph in a single line. Yet these few words, like sweet and silent streams, are eloquently suggestive. They call up a thousand circumstances, over which he must have rejoiced and mourned, and smiled and wept, like the sunshine and showers of an April day.

The name Enoch signifies *teaching*, and was expressive of the office he held as a teacher of the truth. It was his privilege to teach the truth by his life, as well as by his lips. His walk was an excellent homily, and his translation an impressive peroration of it. The doctrines on which he chiefly dwelt, in that early age, were the second advent, the judgment to come, and the resurrection from the dead. "Behold," said he, "the Lord cometh with ten thousand of His saints, to execute judgment upon all, and to convince all that are ungodly among them of all their ungodly deeds, which they have ungodly committed, and of all their hard speeches which ungodly sinners have spoken against Him." These were the topics of prophecy, so awful and so solemn, which he was commissioned to announce. If they were fitted to awe the thoughtless and impenitent, they were equally calculated to afford consolation to believing minds. The heart of the patriarch beat calm and peaceful in the anticipation. There was an unearthliness in his demeanor. The lustre of the Divine countenance was reflected in his person. The radiance of heaven shone around him; and the joys of the upper sanctuary had taken possession of his soul. To one who had risen so rapidly in the scale of future blessedness, the course of nature was for the first time changed, and he was privileged to enter the kingdom by a shorter road. He was *not* ; for God *took him*. God took him at a period when all the patriarchs were living, except Adam, who had been dead about fifty-seven years, — took him in the heyday of life, ere his sun had reached the meridian ; took him in a manner that made his dismissal as glorious to himself, as it was instructive to mankind.

Whether any private intimation had previously been communicated to him of the event, we are not able to determine. We think it highly probable, from the fact, that the Lord generally made known to His servants the purpose of His will. " Shall I hide from Abraham," said He, " the thing which I do ? " On the part of the community at large, there appears to have been no expectation of it; and the discovery must have told with thrilling effect the goodness of God.

Some marvellous change must certainly have

passed over him prior to his translation, as "flesh and blood cannot inherit the kingdom of God." The change was equivalent to death, but without its pain and degradation. The like glorious transformation awaits the living saints at the coming of Christ: "We shall be changed in a moment, in the twinkling of an eye, at the last trump."

There are no processes of nature that can meet the case even by a faint analogy. All the images we can summon to our aid fail to sketch the mere outline of the scene. Were an individual translated from the deepest dungeon into the blaze of noon, — were it possible to bring up some prisoner out of the dark, deep, unfathomable caves of ocean, into the open light and life of creation, — there would be nothing in the incident to compare with the change from the sinfulness of a fallen nature, into the spotless purity and holiness of God; from the gloom and corruption of a body of sin and death, into the spirituality, the light, the life, the glory, the dazzling splendor, that encircle the throne of the Eternal.

The next Ascension occurred many centuries afterward, under a new order of things, in the person of the prophet Elijah, from the banks of the Jordan. Every part of his character was marked by a moral grandeur, heightened by the obscurity thrown around his connections and private history. Clouds and thick darkness covered the scene of his toil, as a reformer in Israel. The images of Baal and Ashteroth, gleamed before the eye. Idolatrous temples and heathen altars occupied the sacred soil; and every valley, and every high hill, smoked with their sacrifices. The man of God, clothed with the panoply of heaven, stood forth in this awful night-piece, to awe the idolatrous by the menace of fearful judgments. In the austerity of his manners, the boldness of his reproofs, and superiority to ease and suffering, he was a striking type of John the Baptist. The forerunner of the Messiah was predicted under his name: " Behold, I will send you Elijah, the prophet, before the coming of the great and dreadful day of the Lord."

When the labors of Elijah were wellnigh

ended, and he had received an intimation of a speedy ascension to the skies, the Spirit of the Lord revealed to him that, before his departure, he was "to anoint Hazael to be king over Syria, and Jehu to be king over Israel, and Elisha, the son of Shaphat, of Abel-meholah, to be prophet in his room." The instructions required him to anoint, without delay, his successor in office; to fill up the post which he himself had so long and toilfully occupied, and to be ready for the Master's summons, "Come up hither." What may we imagine would be the emotions of our own hearts, if such a commission were specifically addressed to us? Could we place in stranger hands, without a struggle, the occupations, and duties, and beings nearest and dearest to us? Could we feel content, and more than content, to resign all at God's bidding, and forsake all for God's presence, and kingdom, and glory? But the prophet, who had dwelt, in anticipation, among holier and happier scenes, showed no hesitation. He was in perfect readiness to lay down his travelling-staff, and bequeath his mantle to another. "So he departed from

Mount Horeb to Abel-meholah," about a hundred and fifty miles distant, and found the object of his pursuit, not wearing "soft raiment," and dwelling in kings' houses, but employed in the arduous and heavy labor of following the plough. "There were twelve yoke of oxen in the field, and Elisha with the twelfth." The venerable father, in God, made his approach to him, and threw the mantle, that was upon his person, over the shoulders of Elisha. Not a word appears to have been spoken at the interview. But Elisha understood its significance, as a consecration to the prophetic office. Instantly he left the oxen, and ran after Elijah, and said, "Let me, I pray thee, kiss my father and my mother, and then I will follow thee." Elijah had no objection to the request, and said, "Go, for what have I done to thee?" I have done nothing which should break ties of affection; I have done nothing to fetter the freedom of thy action. Follow as the Spirit of God shall lead thee. So he turned back from him; and having paid that tribute of respect and affection to his parents, to which he conceived they were entitled, he arose and went after Elijah and ministered unto him. They proceeded together from Gilgal to Bethel, and from Bethel to Jericho, and from Jericho to Jordan. As they stood upon the banks of that mysterious river, "Elijah took his mantle, and with it smote the waters; and they were divided hither and thither, and they two went over on dry ground."

It is with difficulty we can think of the position of the prophet at that solemn moment, without indulging feelings of desire, that the waters of the Jordan of death might be thus happily divided for us. Would that we might escape that fearful passage, in which so many have been engulfed, and pass over dry-shod. There is One, who has declared, "When thou passest through the waters, I will be with thee, and through the floods, they shall not overflow thee." There is One, who has said, "I am the resurrection and the life." " Whosoever liveth and believeth in me, shall never die." "Spare us, Lord, most holy; O God, most mighty; O holy and merciful Saviour. Thou most worthy Judge Eternal, suffer us not, at our last hour, for any pains of death, to fall from thee." Exercise true faith in His atoning merits; cling to Him as loving children; and though you may be called to cross the flood in much tribulation, bodily and mental anguish, your feet shall not sink in those deep waters. You shall stand on the other side, rejoicing, in the language of triumph, we " overcame through the blood of the Lamb."

The master and the servant had travelled together over many a dreary road, and lingered on many a sunny spot; and now, as the period of his translation approached, Elijah requested to be alone, but Elisha as strongly refused to accede to his wish, saying, "As the Lord liveth, and as thy servant liveth, I will not leave thee." Thrice had the desire for solitude been expressed with increased urgency, but Elisha persisted in affirming, "I will not leave thee." It was an interesting moment to both parties; to the man of storm and tempest, just finishing his course; and to his successor in office, just buckling on the armor. The wearisome labors of the day were followed by a placid evening, — an evening tinged with the golden twilight of a blissful world. The horses of fire, and the flaming chariot, were waiting in readiness behind yonder cloud, to fetch him away. The setting sun cast his slanting rays upon him for the last time. And he could say of the stars, as they shone out, one after another, I shall presently pass through those regions, — far beyond the Orion, and the Pleiades, — far beyond the sun, and moon, and realms of space. Dropping all that is mortal, I shall ascend into the very sanctuary of heaven, where cherubim and seraphim worship, and angels strike their harps, and patriarchs dwell in their peaceful tabernacles. I shall mingle with the ancient fathers, I shall see the King in His beauty, and be forever with the Lord.

And "Elijah said unto Elisha, Ask what I shall do for thee, before I be taken away from thee. And Elisha said, I pray thee let a double portion of thy spirit be upon me. And he said, Thou hast asked a hard thing: nevertheless, if thou see me when I am taken from thee, it shall be so unto thee; but if not, it shall not be so.

And it came to pass, as they still went on and talked, that behold there appeared a chariot of fire, and horses of fire, and parted them both asunder, and Elijah went up by a whirlwind into heaven. And Elisha saw it, and he cried, My Father, My Father, the chariot of Israel and the horsemen thereof; and he saw him no more." Thus closed the earthly career of that remarkable man. As we gaze at his fiery chariot, and the bright traces of its ascending wheels, we are impressively taught to set our affections on things above; to covet earnestly the best gifts, and to ask and receive that our joy may be full.

The third and most memorable Ascension was from Mount Olivet. The blessed Jesus had said to His disciples, "It is expedient for you that I go away." "I ascend unto my Father, and your Father, and to my God and your God." Forty days after His resurrection He assembled His Apostles to receive His valedictory. Sad and solemn was the parting interview. While He was yet speaking to them, and their ears drank in His instructions, and their eyes were fixed on His beauty, He was uplifted from among them. They would have clung to Him, but were unable to reach Him. They would have called to Him, but their tongues were fettered with wonder. They sought to follow, with the doting gaze of love, His upward track, but a cloud received Him out of their sight.

<blockquote>" On a bright cloud to heaven He rode."</blockquote>

"And while they looked steadfastly toward heaven as He went up, behold two men stood by them in white apparel. Which also said, Ye men of Galilee, why stand ye gazing up into heaven? this same Jesus which is taken up from you into heaven, shall so come in like manner as ye have seen Him go into heaven." Unlike the translation of Enoch, which no mortal eye was permitted to witness; unlike the ascension of Elijah, whose pathway was the red lightning, and who was borne upward in a whirlwind and chariot of fire, the holy Jesus, when He left the earth, ascended with that quiet majesty, with which He came down to it. The heavenly hosts hailed him as the finisher of a great enterprise. Loud and high were the gratulations He received from all ranks of the glorified. The everlasting doors were thrown open for the King of Glory to enter; and He took His seat " at the right hand of God, in the glory of the Father." The path to the kingdom the Saviour has consecrated by His own presence; made it the beaten track for His redeemed to follow, and left His footprints to say, "This is the way; walk ye in it." It is a path along which none are turned adrift, but cared for in every extremity, ministered to by affectionate intelligences, and conducted by angelic escorts to their final rest.

The three Ascensions teach most distinctly the existence of a better world beyond the grave. They point to better society, better objects, better sounds, intenser splendors, and brighter visions. The land of pure delight has no curse in it, no sickness, no death. Not a leaf fades, not a flower wilts, not a fruit corrupts. On the shores of changelessness there rest no shadows, fall no storms.

The Ascensions of Enoch, Elijah, and Christ,

afford indubitable testimony to the resurrection from the dead. These living personages, as representatives of three different dispensations, having gone up into heaven in a corporeal form, it is but a just and reasonable conclusion that a day is coming when Christ, assuming an aspect of infinite benignity, will call to His sleeping saints to awake in His likeness. This will be a triumph of the highest order, releasing and re-animating what death has dragged away from the territories of the living.

The ascensions assure us that our home is above. The domestic circle is being continually broken on earth; and every break makes it narrower and smaller. The balance soon settles down in the regions of eternity. The centre is removed to the upper sphere. An aged pilgrim at length stands alone on the margin of the river, looking wistfully toward the country of his dearest friends, his most costly treasures, and to which he has been daily taught to give his best affections. The magnet which draws the strongest is the presence of his ascended Lord. The elder brother has gone before to arrange for the arrival and reception of His faithful followers to the same blessed abode. "If ye then be risen with Christ, seek those things which are above." "Set your affections on things above: not on things which are on the earth." Cultivate the moralities of heart and life, which give to heaven its gladness. Be eminent in grace that you may be eminent in glory. Aspire to glorify the Redeemer in some exalted station near the throne. Seek to glow and shine like the seraphim. Prepare for superior distinctions. Lay up rich treasures. Endeavor after an abundant entrance into the everlasting kingdom. Follow hard after God, and thus add a jewel to your crown, and a higher elevation in the scale of majesty and triumph.

# THE THREE MYSTERIOUS UNIONS.

There are mysteries in every department of the Divine procedure; rich veins which have never been explored; paths which the vulture's eye hath not seen, and which are hidden from the view of all living. The origin of moral evil, the lot of individuals, the dissolution of the human frame, the protracted chastisements of the righteous, and the unexampled prosperity of the wicked, are providential enigmas, which the best and wisest of men are unable satisfactorily to explain. There are few truths of Revelation, but are more or less inexplicable. They are partly in the shade, and partly luminous,— seen only at certain angles, and from certain points, and intended principally to exercise our faith. They are parts of a chain, the two ends of which are distinctly seen, while the intermediate links are lost in the stream of mystery that flows between. Certain objects seem presented to the mind, like the sun seen densely through a mist,— at one time appearing, then disappearing,— lost in the thickness of the fog. Sometimes we imagine we see; again our vision is obscured. We only perceive glimmering appearances,— dim outlines. We walk as through a valley, enclosed by lofty mountains, their shadows adding to our obscurities, and their mighty masses standing between us and the prospect which lies beyond. The doctrine of the Holy Trinity is a mystery, which the highest angel is incompetent to unravel. The agency of the Holy Spirit is mysterious. "The wind bloweth where it listeth, and thou hearest the sound thereof; but canst not tell whence it cometh, nor whither it goeth: so is every one that is born of the Spirit."

The three mysterious unions in our holy religion, are the union of the two natures in the Person of our blessed Lord, the mystical union between Christ and His Church, and the union of the Church militant with the Church triumphant. The Bible does not explain the modus of these unions, but simply declares their existence, and leaves to the development of a better and nobler sphere the clearing up of the marvels.

The profoundest of all mysteries, is the mystery of godliness,—"God manifest in the flesh," the complex union of the human and divine natures in Christ, the child born, and the mighty God; the son and the Lord of David; "the root and the offspring of David; the bright and the morning-star." The Holy Jesus possessed the properties of Deity, and inherited the infirmities of humanity; comprised the infinite and the finite, fulness and all-sufficiency, and weariness and want; strength and weakness, life and death. Each nature was distinct, though united; divisible but not divided. The humanity of Christ was as real as His Divinity, and as free from the taint of corruption. A body was prepared for Him: and "He bare our sins in His own body on the tree." He was holy, harmless, undefiled, and separate from sinners." Neither nature was changed by the conjunction, but both retained their peculiar and essential properties intact. In one and the same person,

Christ was the Son of God, and the son of man; supreme, yet a servant; equal with the Father, yet subordinate; rich, yet poor; dignified and exalted, yet humble and abased. The glory of the Godhead was shaded, but not extinguished; obscured, but not lost. As man, Christ prayed to His Father, "with strong crying and tears, and was heard in that He feared." As God, He graciously responded to His beseeching suppliants. As man, He felt hunger, and thirst, and fatigue; as God, He fed many thousands with a few loaves; had the disposal of rivers of living water, and gave rest to the heavy laden and weary. As man, He was tossed on the billowy sea, and slept in a storm; as God, He stilled the raging of the tempest, and brought the drenched mariners to their desired haven. As man, He was crucified, in weakness, and brought into the lowest parts of the earth; as God, He hung all nature in mourning, abolished death, and rose the Resurrection and the Life.

The humiliation of the Lord of glory consisted not so much in laying aside the regalia of heaven for a season, as in cheerfully submitting to a degradation that was perfectly in His power to avoid. Possessed of the prerogatives of Deity, He could have effectually resisted the advances of death, and refused it dominion over His person. But He humbled Himself that the Scriptures might be fulfilled, and because without shedding of blood there could be no remission. To the accursed tree He condescended to be nailed, the wondrous combination of two natures: the one mortal and tending to decay; the other self-existent, and the source of life. The pen of inspiration had predicted that not a bone of Him should be broken; and this was so strictly adhered to in the bitter scene of His death, that, instead of breaking His legs, one of the soldiers with a spear pierced His side, and forthwith came thereout blood and water: blood to redeem, and water to cleanse; the one denoting the efficacy of the atonement, and the other the purification and transformation of our souls, by the washing of regeneration, and the renewing of the Holy Ghost. "This is He that came by water and blood, even Jesus Christ; not by water only, but by water and blood; and it is the Spirit that beareth witness, because the Spirit is truth." The Holy and loving Spirit would have us fix our eye on those sacred streams, which flowed from Immanuel's veins; and as we discover in them the essential blessings of our redemption, to offer to the wounded Saviour, the heartfelt invocation of those sublime stanzas:—

> "Rock of Ages, cleft for me,
> Let me hide myself in thee;
> Let the water and the blood,
> From thy side, a healing flood,
> Be of sin the double cure,—
> Save from wrath and make me pure."

The twofold blessings of salvation and sanctification have their origin in that "fountain opened for sin, and for uncleanness." The one exempts from wrath, the other prepares for heaven. The boon of forgiveness is associated with the process of a daily renewal. And the atoning Saviour, who expiated, on the cross, the guilt of sin, provides for the extirpation of its reigning power, in the washing of water by the word.

The God-man, our Mediator, assures us of the solace of His sympathy. "Because the children were partakers of flesh and blood, He also took part of the same. Himself took our infirmities, and bare our sicknesses." He consented to be like the people He came to redeem, in all points except sinfulness. He was homeless and houseless; maligned, traduced, and slandered; persecuted by enemies, deserted by friends; denied by one apostle, betrayed by another, forsaken by all. His flesh was lacerated by stripes, and torn by nails; His soul was assaulted by temptation, and disquieted under the hidings of His Father's countenance. He could weep with every tear that we weep, except that of repentance; and hope with every hope, and rejoice with every joy that we feel, as men, and as Christians. The roughest path ever trodden was pressed by His sacred feet. The keenest sorrow ever felt was assigned to Him. The bitterest cup ever drank lingered on His lips. The darkest cloud was reserved for Him to penetrate; and the ills of life, the most severe and humiliating, He bore without a murmur. "Verily, He is our companion in tribulation, and our brother in adversity." There is no juniper-tree of the desert, under which we can sit, in pensive solitude, but the meek and lowly Jesus has sat down there many times before us. There are no thorns of the wilderness that can pierce us, which have not pierced His sensitive frame times without number. There are no darts of the adversary that can assail us, but have afflicted Him in the fiercest form. The most oppressed, betrayed, and forsaken, must feel that he has one friend who can sympathize, whose soul was exceeding sorrowful, even unto death. Never was our nature honored with a being so affectionate and sympathetic; so full of dignity, and majesty, and loveliness, and tenderness, and softness. His word so powerful, His touch so healing, His smile so heavenly. Jesus is "the chief among ten thousand, the altogether lovely."

Only a personage thus constituted, very God and very man, was adequate to the mighty work of redemption. The breach of sin no arm of flesh could heal. It was a chasm which the wings of human love could not cross, and which the feet of human devotedness could not wade. The omnipotent Saviour alone could span the tremendous gulf, and so of twain make one by the blood of the cross.

The mystical union of Christ and His Church is so indissoluble and glorious, that it will be best understood in the light of eternity. "At that day," said Christ, "ye shall know that I am in the Father, and ye in Me, and I in you." The perfect vision shall show how much there is of God and Christ bound up in the Church. Her beauty and order are but reflections of the transcendent glory and preciousness of Him whose Church she is, in whose righteousness she is clothed, and in whose comeliness she is comely. The universe has neither grandeur, nor sublimity in His eye, in comparison with the Church, which He has purchased with His blood. The Redeemer has embarked His glory in her salvation, and is wont to reveal Himself in a thousand ways, that will fill all holy intelligences with admiration forever. She is His Spouse, His Body, His fulness, the almoner of

His bounty, to dispense the treasures of grace to the children of men. Every baptized convert to Christ is a member of the Church, born through the labors of the Church, nourished by the instructions of the Church, watched over, and trained for heaven, by the discipline of the Church. The Church is the birthplace of saints. "The Lord shall count, when He writeth up the people, that this man was born there." The last and best gift of heaven to the Church was the ministry of reconciliation, "for the perfecting of the saints, for the edifying of the Body of Christ, till we all come to the unity of the faith, and of the knowledge of the Son of God, unto a perfect man, unto the measure of the stature of the fulness of Christ." This, the Holy Spirit tells us, was the object which the Son of God had in view, when He instituted the different orders of the ministry. "The treasure was put in earthen vessels, that the excellency of the power might be of God, and not of us." Deprive the Church of her ministry, and all other agencies for good would wither away. Zeal for the truth would languish. Efforts of religious usefulness would cease. The light of the holy Sabbath would go out. The ten thousand benefits of Christianity would be lost, because her solemn feasts are not celebrated, her altars are not honored, and her tidings are not proclaimed. The day would be turned into night, and the garden of the Lord into a wilderness and solitary place. Whatever is glorious and godlike, is the fruit of the ministry of the Church, as founded on the Apostles and Prophets, Jesus Christ himself being the chief cornerstone. The Lord who decreed that the earth should have no day, but by the shining of the sun, has alike ordained that the world shall have no spiritual illumination, but by reflection from His Church, and His Church no source of blessing but through the agency of her ministry, which, like the mystic lamps of the tabernacle, He hath set up in the midst of the sanctuary.

The world owes its existence to the Church. She is instrumentally and subordinately its moral preservation and glory. Take her away from the earth, and what remains but a mass of unmitigated evil, a world of unrelieved corruption, an empire wholly in rebellion against God, and in subjection to Satan?— The salt extracted, the light extinguished, the wheat sifted from the chaff, the gold separated from the dross, and nought is left but fuel for the fearful and final conflagration. Such is the doom that awaits the earth, when it shall cease to be the dwelling-place of the faithful.

On common principles of reasoning, a very long continuance of the Church might be deemed almost impossible, since she finds in every man a natural and inveterate foe. But "the Lord her God in the midst of her is mighty." "Her life is hidden with Christ in God." It grows with the quickening of the heart, and unfolds itself in "righteousness and peace, and joy in the Holy Ghost." Were she an earthly element, striving to neutralize a rival, she might be absorbed in her own; but she is of heavenly parentage, and inextinguishable vitality, assimilating earth to heaven, and man to God. Her union with Christ is the union of the bride with the bridegroom. "I am married unto you, saith the Lord." "Thy

Maker is thy husband, the Lord of Hosts is His name." "He that hath the bride is the bridegroom: as the bridegroom rejoiceth over the bride, so shall thy God rejoice over thee." "Husbands love your wives, as Christ also loved the Church, and gave Himself for it."

Is there union between the head and the body? Christ is "the Head of His body, the Church"; and we are "members of His body, of His flesh, and of His bones." "The body is not one member, but many, and God hath set the members, every one as it hath pleased Him." The eyes see for the body; the hands handle for the body; the feet walk for the body; the palate tastes for the body; the nerves feel for body. They are all component parts of one and the same system, acting in concert through one common organization; the members many, the body one. "By one Spirit we are all baptized into one body." The Holy Spirit is given to the body, the Church, that in her capacious bosom there may be but one heart to sway its motions, and direct its actions; a heart that shall beat in unison with heaven, and whose every impulse shall diffuse life, and health, and joy to the remotest members. The Spirit of spirits, yea the fountain spirit, as a living soul animates, cements, and pervades the whole. As God is said to have taken of the spirit that was in Moses, and put it upon the seventy elders, so He takes of the spirit that was in Christ, and puts it upon His disciples. And as the holy oil, with which Aaron was anointed, was first poured in richest profusion on the head, and thence flowed to the lowest borders and fringes of his garments, the rich unction poured upon Christ descends to the least and lowest of the members of His mystical body.

The incorporation of His people into Himself, the gracious Saviour beautifully illustrates under the additional similitude of the vine and the branches. "I am the vine," says He; "ye are the branches. As the branch cannot bear fruit of itself, except it abide in the vine, no more can ye, except ye abide in Me." The condition of life and fertility is being in Christ; one with Him, partakers of the divine nature, and recipients of His gracious influences. The juice of the parent stock is the same in the numerous branches; and the members of Christ's body have one common life with Him, and with the several individual parts, of which His body consists. This is mentioned by St. Paul as a motive not to speak, or act to the injury of a fellow-Christian, because being members one of another, any wound that we inflict on a brother, is violence done to our own spiritual life, and to the body as a whole. One can hardly expect any branch of the true vine to grow and prosper, while in irritating collision with adjacent ones. Certainly no part of the human frame is strengthened by inflicting a blow on it. The hand weakens itself when it inflicts pain on the foot. And if we act bitterly or uncharitably toward those who are fellow-heirs of the grace of life, we not only violate that common sympathy, by which the members of Christ's body participate in one common hope, but we turn from us the heart, and approbation of Christ, from whom our life is derived. As one in Christ Jesus, it behooves us to " endeavor to keep the unity of the Spirit, in the bond of peace."

The living body of the Lord comprehends the unseen world. The visible and the invisible are connected by the same presiding Head, " of whom the whole family in heaven and earth is named." He is the bond of union to the Church, militant and triumphant. The communion of saints brings us into association with the blessed in heaven. "Ye are come," said the Apostle, "unto Mount Zion, and unto the city of the living God, the heavenly Jerusalem, and to an innumerable company of angels, to the general assembly and church of the first-born, which are written in heaven, and to God the Judge of all, and to the spirits of just men made perfect, and to Jesus the Mediator of the new covenant." Whether in the body, or out of the body, the fellowship of holy minds is attracted to one common centre, dear alike to the one, and the other.

> " Angels, and living saints, and dead
> But one communion make;
> All join in Christ, their living Head,
> And of His love partake."

The cold hand of death is powerless to separate.

spirits so closely cemented. If the dissolution of the human frame causes any change in the relation of the souls of the living to those of the departed, it must consist in the enlarging and strengthening of former intimacy. Did you love the lost one for the lineaments of the Saviour's image impressed on the heart? Then the tie was not merely one of flesh and blood, but of spirit, which still exists. The foundation that originally formed the basis of your fellowship, remains unimpaired. The golden chain which binds soul to soul, and both to heaven, continues ever. Give then to the earth her tribute, the dust to dust, and commune with the soul, which God has taken, in the unity of the spirit, the communion of saintship in the Lord. The dead in Christ are the spirits of the just made perfect. Their imperfections have ceased. Their faculties are more vigorous than when shut up in the body; the memory is more awake; the sensibilities are quicker. We can neither see, nor hear them. This would be inconsistent with the arrangements of Providence, which require that we walk by faith. But the fragrance of their virtues steals over us like the soft pulsations of a south wind, laden with the sweets of a new-mown field. " The memory of the just is blessed." Sometimes we feel as though we were sailing away from them; but we are sailing towards them; they are gone to preoccupy the home, to which we are aspiring, and we are nearer to them now, than yesterday: the night is far spent; the day is at hand.

The blessed thought, that we are counted worthy to be admitted to such a fellowship, made partakers of such privileges, and inheritors of such a kingdom, should fill our hearts with love and gratitude, and deeply humble us with a sense of our utter unworthiness. It should kindle higher aspirations after communion with Christ, excite more fervent longings for holiness, and heavenly mindedness, and dispose us to a waiting attitude for the peace, and purity, and harmony of heaven.

The voyage of life hastens to its close with amazing rapidity. We shall soon hear the rasping on the shallows, and the commotion overhead, which bespeak the port in view.

Gliding through breaking shadows, and softly unfolding light, we shall merge into the open vision of things unseen and eternal: not violently, like being whirled instantly into a distant city, and then waking up amid the confusion and strangeness of the place. The heavenly Jerusalem appears first in the distance. The approach to it is gradual. Sweet voices are heard afar off. Celestial forms whisper peace to the soul:—

> "Hark! they whisper; angels say,
> Sister spirit, come away."

Jesus vouchsafes His cheering presence,— pillows the languid head upon His bosom,—speaks words of cheer to the struggling, panting soul,— bids the tempter make no menace,—causes overshadowing splendors to fall around, and ministers an abundant entrance into the full sunshine, and perfect realization and enjoyment of His full-orbed glories in the everlasting kingdom. The three mysterious unions will then cease to be seen through a glass darkly. They are interesting pictures, with infinite lines in them, eminently calculated to lead us to love and adore. We wait with hope and patience for the dawn of the era, when perfect light shall solve every mystery, and " we shall know, even as also we are known." Change and vicissitude we expect in all sublunary things, but not in the holy mysteries of Christ, and His Church. These are not fictions, but truths; not gorgeous descriptions, but consolations; not enchanting narratives, but the irrefragable, settled and eternal verities of faithfulness itself. They are realities which endure, when the romance of life shall cease, — solid, unyielding rock, that has been tried, and tested, and sifted with the strictest scrutiny, and has never been found wanting, — the rock of God's faithfulness and love, upon which serenely reposing, we can look up to Him, in our last moments, and say with confidence, " O Lord, in thee have I trusted, let me never be confounded."

## THE THREE IN ONE.

The doctrine of a Trinity in Unity, is one of pure revelation. Philosophy with its splendid discoveries has shed no illumination on the subject. It was reserved for Christianity to restore and establish the truth in its original purity. We have analogies in a thousand forms, which cannot fail to impress us. There is a Trinity in LIGHT, which affords an admirable illustration of this article of our faith. It was believed for many ages that light consisted of seven component parts; but a more thorough investigation into its laws and properties has decided that it properly comprises only three. The red, yellow, and blue, are the primary, or essential colors, from which all the others are derived. Thus, orange is found between the red and yellow; and green, between the yellow and blue; so that in reality we have but three original colors to deal with, each of which has its own peculiar attributes. The calorific or heating principle is found in the red, the luminous or light-giving principle in the yellow, and the power of chemical action in the blue. Under the influence of the two former, plants will live and grow luxuriantly; but they will bear no fruit without the enlivening power of the blue ray. Life is unproductive until the three united in one bring all things to perfection. It is the trinity of red, yellow, and blue, which constitutes, when combined, the unity of ordinary, or white light. The three are one, and the one is three, exhibiting a trinity in unity, and a unity in trinity.

There is a trinity in WATER,—the fountain, the stream, and the mist. The fountain, high up among the hills, answers to the Father; the stream which issues from the fountain, and flows down into the valley below, corresponds with the Son; and the mist which rises from the water, and descends upon the thirsty earth in showers of rain or dew, being a fit emblem of the Holy Spirit. This was a favorite similitude under which He was predicted by the prophets: "He shall come down like rain upon the mown grass, and as showers that water the earth." "I will be as the dew unto Israel, and he shall grow as the lily."

There is a trinity in LANGUAGE. We discover in the dialects of all nations but three persons, each one suggestive of the other. The first involves the second, and the second the third. Whether singular, or plural, there is no fourth person. The whole is simply a repetition of the first three. There is therefore in human speech something like a shadowy outline of the doctrine of the Holy Trinity. An illustration of similar import is occasionally drawn from the constitution of our nature. The ancients used to define the complex being of man as composed of body, soul, and spirit; three component parts, constituting one and the same person. But little stress deserves to be placed in these allusions, as they are not proofs, only intimations, of the sublime reality, which defies all human comprehension.

The existence of a plurality of persons in the

Godhead is definitely presented us in the first and second verses of the first chapter of the Book of Genesis: "In the beginning God created the heaven and the earth. And the earth was without form, and void: and darkness was upon the face of the deep. And the Spirit of God moved upon the face of the waters." The Hebrew word for God is used in the plural number, and the word *created* in the singular; the one pointing to a plurality of persons, and the other to their unity. The Eternal Father is presented to us as the Omnipotent Creator of all things; the everlasting Son is the *logos*, or word, that was in the beginning with God, and without whom nothing was made that was made. And the Holy Spirit is revealed as moving on the surface of the deep, brooding over, fluttering, like a dove, and infusing into the vast abyss the principle of life. The whole Trinity is collectively embodied in the expression, *Bara Elohim*, the Gods created. So deeply was this truth impressed on the mind of the great Hebrew legislator, that there is scarcely any other method of speaking, from which a plurality in Deity may be inferred, that is not used either by himself in the Pentateuch, or by other inspired writers in various parts of the Old Testament. If the combining of this plural noun with a verb in the singular occurred only once, it might be supposed to be an accidental violation of grammar; but as it is employed about thirty times in the concise history of the creation, and in those portions of Holy Writ where the creation is alluded to, the design was evidently to establish at the outset a theological system, of which the unity of the Trinity was the leading feature. We read of Jacob, that he called the name of the place Bethel, because the Gods there appeared to him. We read in Joshua, "Ye cannot serve the Lord: for He is the Holy Gods." And there is that remarkable passage in the Book of Ecclesiastes, "Remember now thy Creators in the days of thy youth." The Jews argue, that these numerous examples imply the existence of more than one person in the Godhead; and the Church universal has decided, that they are an intimation of the glorious truth of a triune Jehovah.

The twenty-sixth verse of the first chapter of Genesis, affords another argument equally conclusive. "And God said, Let us make man in onr image, after our likeness." The proposition, we think, is so pointed an attestation of plurality, that, when duly and rightly considered, it must stagger the most hardened sceptic. Quotations of this complexion we could cite in abundance, demonstrating most beautifully the manner in which the Most High speaks of himself as more than one : " And the Lord God said, Behold the man is become like one of *us*." " And the Lord said, Let *us* go down, and there confound their language." " I heard the voice of the Lord, saying, Whom shall I send, and who will go for us?" "And now the Lord God, and His Spirit hath sent me." "By the word of the Lord were the heavens made, and all the host of them by the breath of His mouth." " Seek ye out of the book of the Lord, and read : for my mouth it hath commanded : and His Spirit, it hath gathered them." Whether God the Father, or God the Son, be the speaker, in the last mentioned passage, it is not material to determine, as the whole Trinity is evidently included. So it would also seem, in the triple benediction pronounced by the High-Priest, as recorded in the fourth chapter of Numbers: "The Lord bless thee, and keep thee. The Lord make His face to shine upon thee, and be gracious unto thee. The Lord lift up His countenance upon thee, and give thee peace." The three separate blessings invoked belong, respectively, to the three persons in the Godhead, in the order of the Father, Son, and Spirit: the Father being the source of blessing and preservation; the Saviour, the author of grace and illumination; and the Holy Spirit, the Comforter, and giver of peace.

Turn we now to the New Testament for some of the proofs which it meets with there. The doctrine of the Holy Trinity is most explicitly revealed in the commission, which the Lord gave to His Apostles, after His resurrection: "Go ye therefore and teach all nations, baptizing them in the name of the Father, and of the Son, and of the Holy Ghost." The administration of the rite agreeably to the prescribed formula, supposes no inferiority in the persons of the Trinity, but that the three are of one substance, power, and perfection; all equally concurring in the great plan of human redemption. The Saviour's own baptism tended beautifully to place this truth beyond all doubt. When He had fulfilled all righteousness on the banks of the Jordan, His conduct met with the approval of the Holy Three. The Father testified His pleasure in His approving voice; the Son, in His illustrious example; and the Holy Spirit, in His visible descent.

In the name of the blessed Trinity we were baptized into the Church, and thus taught that the work of our salvation is so vast that it brings into action every distinctive attribute of the Divine nature, causing the triune Jehovah to find ample scope for the employment of every perfection, and the affluence of every grace. In that solemn hour, when the outward and visible sign of inward and spiritual grace fell upon our countenances, we were set apart and claimed for God. We are the property of the Trinity. Each person of the Deity has an interest in us, and to each we must surrender ourselves by an entire and appropriate consecration. If our obligations before were infinite, what must we think of them now, on beholding three distinct subsistences actually confederating and conferring together, and embarking the treasuries of heaven in the cause of our happiness? Surely an ocean of felicity is placed before sinful beings, whose hearts scarcely overflow with a drop.

The doxology of St. Paul, at the conclusion of his Second Epistle to the Corinthians, is another proof equally pertinent: "The grace of our Lord Jesus Christ, and the love of God, and the communion of the Holy Ghost be with you all. Amen." This Apostolic benediction is found at the close of Morning and Evening Prayer, and fitly applies to every period of time. The three great blessings of grace, love, and fellowship, are sought, respectively, from Jesus Christ, God the Father, and the Holy Ghost, as equal in essence, will, power, and glory, and every perfection.

The invocations in the Litany are made distinctly to each separate person of the Deity, and then to the Three in One. We acknowledge the glory of the Eternal Trinity, and worship the Unity. This occasions no distraction of thought, or fearful apprehension, of not worshipping each person in due proportion. We need but to lift up our hearts in true faith, and adoring love; and whether we address the Father, or the Son, we pray to one and the same God, who is over all, blessed forever. The primitive Christians prayed mostly to Christ. They were distinguished by the practice of calling on the name of the Lord Jesus. It is the will and purpose of God that at the name of Jesus every knee shall bow. In paying Him homage, we give glory to the Father; and in honoring the Holy Spirit, we honor the Father and the Son, from whom the Spirit proceeds. Whether we exercise our best affections on the ever-loving Jehovah, as the fountain of life and happiness; or on the lovely Redeemer, who wrought out for us the blessings of everlasting salvation; or on the Comforter and Revealer, who fills us with joy and peace in believing, we know that we love the Lord, as the one great object of worship, and have a just appreciation of His mercies in the plan of human redemption.

> "Now teach my lips to sing on earth,
> And meekly set Thy praises forth,
> The songs which choirists sing in heaven,
> From holy themes which Thou hast given.
> The Three in One, the One in Three,
> Who was, and is, and yet shall be,—
> The wondrous, glorious mystery,
> The song of all eternity."

The doctrine of the Trinity is the doctrine of the divinity of Jesus Christ. The blessed Jesus Himself taught it, when He declared, "I and my Father are one." St. Peter says, "He is Lord of All" The Church, with one consent, lifts up her voice in the Nicene Creed, "I believe in one Lord, Jesus Christ, the only-begotten Son of God, begotten of His Father before all worlds: God of God, Light of Light, very God of very God." She chants His Deity in her lofty *Te Deum,*—"Thou art the King of glory, O Christ." Also in that inimitable song, *The Gloria in excelsis*, she sings, "Thou only art Holy. Thou only art the Lord. Thou only, O Christ, with the Holy Ghost, art most high, in the glory of God the Father."

The mystery of the Three in One is recorded as a matter of faith; but it is not given to us to know in what manner the three are united, and how separately and jointly they are God. Our finite comprehensions are too limited to grasp the nature and properties of an infinite Being. "Who by searching can find out God? Who can find out the Almighty to perfection?" God is a Spirit, and man's gross perceptions are but ill adapted to the understanding of a spiritual essence. "If I have told you earthly things," said Christ, "and ye receive them not, how shall ye believe if I tell you of heavenly things?" "Such knowledge is too wonderful and excellent for us: it is high, we cannot attain unto it: the measure thereof is larger than the earth, and broader than the sea." The most gifted intelligence, if placed in the immediate presence of Deity; if endowed with all the powers that heaven and earth can supply; and if employed in the most diligent research for ages innumerable, would know no more of the triune Jehovah than a mariner knows of the ocean, which he can neither measure, nor fathom. Were he to take the universe orb by orb, and travel from star to star, from sun to sun, and from system to system,—were he to see and comprehend all that God has made,—he would feel so overpowered with the discovery of wisdom, majesty, and splendor blazing around, that there would remain no life in him. Our duty is to receive with docility the testimony which God has given; and to fix our footing upon that firmest of all foundations, and most rational of all evidences, "Thus saith the Lord."

The benefit of a revelation of the doctrine of a Trinity in Unity is the knowledge of what God has done for us. But for this, we should have known nothing of God's Fatherly character; nothing of the Saviour's sympathy; nothing of the history of the Comforter. We should have felt ourselves orphan children, friendless and desolate.

To faithful and believing souls there is much to console in this article of faith. The unity of salvation requires the eye to be fixed principally on one object,—the central person of the Godhead,—"Believe on the Lord Jesus Christ, and thou shalt be saved." Look to Him amidst your embarrassments and depressions; and like the roving dove, sweeping with drooping wing the troubled waters, and finding no repose until, weary and panting, she behies herself to the ark, so in that one blessed and precious object your fluttering and believing heart shall find rest and peace. The thoughts, distracted and perturbed, cluster around the Trinity like so many children anxious to reciprocate the love of an affectionate parent. Here they find a resting-place from their wanderings: the bands of worldliness are unloosed, and we live in the enjoyment of holy influences girding us for duty. The Lord only can heal the troubled waters of the heart. He only can purify the sub-springs of the soul, and turn the turbid fountain into sweetness of purity and brightness. He only can give that direction to the thoughts that shall make them a well of water, springing up into everlasting life.

www.ingramcontent.com/pod-product-compliance
Lightning Source LLC
Chambersburg PA
CBHW021355230426
43666CB00006B/530